GOD'S
MASTERPLAN

GOD'S MASTERPLAN

penetrating the mystery of Christ

PETER HOCKEN

Alive Publishing

First published in 2003 by Alive Publishing Ltd.
Graphic House, 124 City Road, Stoke on Trent ST4 2PH
Tel: +44 (0) 1782 745600. Fax: +44 (0) 1782 745500
www.biblealive.co.uk e-mail:editor@biblealive.co.uk

©2003 Alive Publishing
British Library Catalogue-in-Publication Data. A
catalogue record for this book is available from the
British Library.

ISBN 0-9540335-3-1

CONTENTS

INTRODUCTION

This book is about the secret of God, the mystery that God makes known through the Holy Spirit. It is the secret about his Son, the kingdom and the bride. These are intimately connected. The kingdom of God is closely bound up with Jesus himself, and the Church is his beloved. Why write about God's secret or mystery? Because this is what God most wants to communicate to his beloved.

God seeks to deliver us from our self-absorption to enter into the plan and vision that shapes all that he has done from the first moment of creation. In our own religious worlds, our focus easily dwells on what God is doing for us. When people experience conversion to Jesus Christ, there is naturally an awareness of the majesty of Jesus, but our understanding is often limited by our self-focus. This self-focus may not be selfish in the narrowly personal sense, but it may be more a focus on the graces being given than a focus on the heart of the Father.

Even in the beginnings of the Church, we find that the initial message is about what Jesus has done for us, about what God has done for us in and through his Son. But then the Holy Spirit leads the Church deeper into the Father's heart. The gift of faith lifts up the church community to see everything through the eyes of God. This process is seen especially in the letters of Paul and in the gospel of John. Everything - concerning Jesus, concerning the Church, concerning the world - can be understood in the light of the eternal plan of God centred on his Son. The good news of the gospel becomes the revelation of the secret of God, the mystery of Christ.

Two years ago *Alive Publishing* published my book *Blazing the Trail*, which reflected on the theme 'Where is the Holy Spirit leading the Church?' It arose from the experience within Catholic charismatic renewal of finding many who had experienced a renewal of faith and who had discovered a vitality and an enthusiasm they had not known before, but who still had little idea of where this renewal was leading. In other words, they lacked vision.

In many ways *God's Masterplan* is a sequel to *Blazing the Trail*. The focus of *Blazing the Trail* was on the renewing work of the Holy Spirit in the contemporary Church: the Church being made more evangelistic, more eucharistic, more ecumenical and more eschatological. *God's Masterplan* goes directly to the biblical word that more than any other expresses God's vision for the world and the Church: *mystērion*, generally translated as 'mystery', though sometimes as 'secret'.

In the Christian world, there are two sharply contrasting attitudes to 'mystery'. Among Christians from liturgical traditions with an emphasis on the sacraments, 'mystery' is a familiar term. Catholics speak of the mystery of the holy Trinity, the mystery of the incarnation, the mystery of the holy eucharist. We also speak of the paschal mystery, referring to the passover of Jesus from this world to the Father through his passion, death and resurrection. After the consecration at each

Mass in the Roman rite, the priest invites the people to proclaim 'the mystery of faith'.

In common Catholic understanding, mystery refers to a truth or reality that is inaccessible to human reason on its own, and that can only be known by divine revelation. The *Catechism of the Catholic Church*, citing the First Vatican Council of 1870, says: 'The Trinity is a mystery of faith in the strict sense, one of the "mysteries that are hidden in God, which can never be known unless they are revealed by God".'

As we shall see, the New Testament concept of mystery is not quite the same as the common Catholic understanding. This is not to say that the received Catholic view is an aberration. The Catholic understanding is derived from the biblical view, but in the course of its development some elements in the biblical view have receded into the background. The recovery of these neglected elements forms part of the biblical renewal that is necessary both for the renewal of the Church and for the restoration of Christian unity.

In contrast to Catholic usage, 'mystery' is a term largely absent from Evangelical Protestant discourse. Despite its biblical character, mystery represents for most Evangelicals a fear of things Catholic: it suggests bells and smells, vestments and ritual, in a word 'superstition' rather than truth. Mystery for the Evangelical can savour of religious confusion among those who have not received the clear light of the gospel. It is an eloquent example of how the conflict of division can distort the vision of both sides. The bias of conflict can alone explain how a biblical concept such as mystery could be neglected by Evangelical Christians who are so devoted to the Bible. In this ecumenical age of greater humility and repentance, we Catholics need to recognize how our behaviour can feed this Evangelical fear.

The argument of *God's Masterplan* is that there is a common element in the biblical use of the term 'mystery' and that, for the apostle Paul, mystery expresses the eternal plan or vision of the Father centred on his Son, Jesus the Christ. Thus, the question asked in *Blazing the Trail* - where is the Holy Spirit leading the Church? - was answered there in terms of the experience of the new ecclesial movements, the renewal of biblical scholarship and the contemporary magisterium of the Church. In

God's Masterplan, the same question is answered from the Scriptures by examining the rich connotations of mystery or secret in the New Testament.

Peter Hocken
Vienna, July 2003

Part I

The Gospel of the Kingdom

THE MYSTERY OF THE KINGDOM

To you has been given the secret of the kingdom of God (Mk 4:11)

In the New Testament, 'mystery' is not one of the most common terms. Words like kingdom, repentance, faith, salvation, and *parousia*[1] are far more frequent. But 'mystery' has a particular importance that will form the subject of this book. 'Mystery' is a key term for understanding the whole message of the Sacred Scriptures and for entering into the fullness of divine revelation.

Mystery in the Gospels

This reflection on 'mystery' begins with the Gospels. This is not simply because the teaching of Jesus came before the teaching of the apostles, but because, as the *Catechism of the Catholic Church* says: 'The Gospels are the heart of all the

Scriptures'.[2] The reason is that 'they are our principal source for the life and teaching of the Incarnate Word, our Saviour.' In the Catholic liturgy, we express our particular reverence for the words of the Gospels by standing when the Gospel is proclaimed.

The Gospels present the life and teaching of Jesus. Jesus is the Messiah of Israel, the beloved Son of the Father. His words possess a depth that no subsequent disciple can match. While the epistles of the New Testament open up the teaching of Jesus and have a strong appeal to the teachers and preachers of clear doctrine, it is the life and teaching of Jesus presented in the Gospels that grounds the whole New Testament. It is the narrative and encounter character of the Gospels that allows the eternal and the infinite to break into the human without reduction or distortion.

In the Gospels, 'mystery' occurs only once, but this unique occasion is rather important. It comes in the three synoptic Gospels at the point where Jesus begins to teach in parables. His disciples ask him about the parables, wondering why he is teaching in this way. Jesus replies: 'To you has been given the secret [*mystērion*] of the kingdom of God, but for those outside everything is in parables' (Mark 4:11). A similar wording is found in the parallel passages in Matthew 13:11 and Luke 8:10, where the words of Jesus use the plural, speaking of the 'mysteries' or 'secrets' of the kingdom.

These are verses that we easily skip over. Maybe we are put off by the enigmatic statements that follow: 'This is why I speak to them in parables, because seeing they do not see, and hearing they do not hear, nor do they understand.' (Matt. 13:13). As regular churchgoers we become dulled to the parables, hearing them so often. It is hard to recapture the impact on those who first heard them from the lips of Jesus.

A point we easily miss is that these passages provide a key for understanding the whole teaching of Jesus. His teaching is about the kingdom: the kingdom of heaven in Matthew, the kingdom of God in Mark and Luke. The Jewish people expected the coming of the kingdom. This hope was linked with the coming of the Messiah, the one anointed by God to be king over Israel. As a son of David, he would restore the kingdom to Israel. The angel Gabriel had promised Mary about her son: 'the Lord God will give to him the throne of his father David, and he will reign over the house of Jacob for ever' (Luke 1:32-33). Some thirty years later, just before the beginning of the ministry of Jesus, John the Baptist announced the imminence of the kingdom: 'Repent, for the kingdom of heaven is at hand.' (Matt. 3:2).

Why does Jesus speak of the kingdom as 'mystery' or 'mysteries'? First, it would seem that Jesus wanted to disabuse the Jewish people of simplistic views about the coming of the kingdom. It would not just be a 'restoration' - a return of the kingdom to Israel as it had existed in the days of King David. It would be something of a different order, way beyond the Jewish political expectations at that time.

Second, Jesus was tapping into a strain of Jewish thinking that is called 'apocalyptic'. 'Apocalyptic', which comes from the Greek word to 'unveil', means the unveiling or revelation of something previously hidden. The word 'mystery' occurred in this sense in the book of Daniel (see Dan. 2:18): 'Blessed be the name of God for ever and ever .... He reveals deep and mysterious things' (Dan. 2:20, 22). 'Mystery' was found in several Jewish books in the inter-testamental period between the Old and the New Testaments. In the book of Enoch, the visionary author writes: 'For I know this mystery; I have read the tablets of heaven and have seen the holy writings, and I have understood the writing in them' (104:10). In these apocalyptic writings, 'mystery' refers to the final realization of God's plan, that is now unveiled and made known to his chosen ones. So when Jesus says the secret(s) or mystery(ies) of the kingdom is being revealed to the disciples, he is saying that his teaching reveals the hidden plan of God that is even now coming to realization.

The Parables

When Jesus speaks of mystery, it is linked to his teaching in parables. At first sight, it might seem that he only teaches in parables to those who are incapable of hearing his message, but that to the disciples 'he speaks clearly'. The implication is certainly that the teaching of Jesus can only be understood by an enlightened heart (see Matt. 13: 15). In fact, Jesus teaches everyone in parables, but to the disciples he explains their meaning. 'With many such parables he spoke the word to them, as they were able to hear it; he did not speak to them without a parable, but privately to his disciples he explained everything' (Mark 4:33-34).

Because the parables are so rich and varied, evoking so many images and touching on so many themes, we easily forget the thread that unites them all: the kingdom. The parables are about the kingdom. For the Jews, the image of the kingdom was concrete. Kingdom was not a vague or abstract concept. It did not just refer to a future condition, much less to a mere state of mind, or to people's attitudes. The Jewish people expected and longed for the Messiah-King, whose coming would transform everything - personal, social, political, cultural. We see this expectation in Simeon who, 'righteous and devout, looking for the consolation of Israel' (Luke 2:25), was led to recognize 'the Lord's Messiah'. We see it also in Anna, who spoke of the infant Jesus to 'all who were looking for the redemption of Jerusalem' (Luke 2:38).

Many of the parables refer to someone in authority: a king 'who wished to settle accounts with his servants' (Matt. 18:23); a householder 'who went out to hire labourers for his vineyard' (Matt. 20:1); 'a householder who planted a vineyard' (Matt. 21:33); 'a king who gave a marriage feast for his son' (Matt. 22:2); 'a man going on a journey [who] called his servants and entrusted to them his property' (Matt. 25:14); 'a man who gave a great banquet and invited many' (Luke 14:16); 'a judge who neither feared God nor regarded man' (Luke 18:2). These parables almost all concern the behaviour of the servants or subjects and how they are treated by the one in authority. They reveal characteristics of the rule of God, of God's generosity and of God's justice.

The parables speak both of the kingdom and of the king. The message of the kingdom remained concrete as long as there was a focus on the coming of the king. While the Catholic Church has celebrated a feast of Christ the King since 1925, the preface for the feast speaks more abstractly of the coming kingdom: 'an eternal and universal kingdom, a kingdom of truth and life, a kingdom of holiness and grace, a kingdom of justice, love and peace'. It is only as descriptions of the kingdom are complemented by the promise of the Lord's coming in glory that the kingdom of God is no longer abstract and idealistic. The hope of the personal coming of the king is more clearly expressed in the prefaces for Advent, such as: 'Now we watch for the day, hoping that the salvation promised us will be ours when Christ our Lord will come again in his glory.'

Sons of the Kingdom

Only for the first two parables concerning the
sowing of seed does Jesus give a detailed
explanation of their meaning. The first is the
parable of the sower, whose seed falls on different
kinds of ground: on the path, on rocky ground, on
thorns and on good soil (Matt. 13:3-9). The second
is the parable of the field in which both good seed
and weeds are sown (Matt. 13:24-30). It is
significant that the first two parables in the
Gospels for which explanations are provided teach
us both about the reception of the seed and about
the ultimate harvest.

First, the seed is sown. The first parable addresses
directly the immediate fate of the seeds. With the
planting of seeds, there is a time of hidden growth
before the shoots appear. The first parable makes
clear the difference made by the soil (shallow or
good) and by the environment (thorns or no thorns).
The explanation shows that Jesus is focused on the
final harvest: 'As for what was sown on good soil,
this is he who hears the word and understands it;
he indeed bears fruit, and yields, in one case a
hundredfold, in another sixty, and in another thirty'
(Matt. 13:23).

This conclusion is even more clear from the second parable. Here the problem is not the wrong soil, but the weeds. Jesus warns the disciples against uprooting the weeds lest the wheat also be pulled up. The separation will only come at the time of harvest, when the wheat will be gathered into the barns and the weeds will be burned. In the first parable, the seed is the word of God (Mark 4:14), and in the second there is an allusion to Jesus as the sower: 'He who sows the good seed is the Son of man' (Matt. 13:37).

Jesus is always concerned with the immediate response, and he is also looking to the final destiny. The parables of the kingdom always contain an immediate challenge, but many also speak of the final fulfilment. So in the second parable, Jesus says: 'Just as the weeds are gathered and burned with fire, so will it be at the close of the age (*en té synteleía tou aiōnos*).' (Matt. 13:40). 'Then the righteous will shine like the sun in the kingdom of their Father.' (Matt. 13:43). From the start 'the good seed means the sons of the kingdom' (Matt. 13:38), but they will only reach their glorious destiny 'at the close of the age' - with Jesus hinting at the bodily resurrection in the image of 'shining like the sun'.

Through this parable, Jesus invites us to grasp the promise of the final or fulfilled kingdom. Only as we receive what it means to be 'sons of the kingdom' who 'will shine like the sun in the kingdom of their Father' do we truly grasp the character of the seed already sown. A seed already contains its final destiny. We are already sons or daughters, but we do not yet see the future glory of God's family.

Hiddenness and Revelation

The message of Jesus about the kingdom always touches on this relationship between the present and the future. There is a challenge now and a pledge for the future. There is a presence of the kingdom that even now prepares for the future fullness. When the Pharisees ask Jesus when the kingdom of God is coming, he replies: 'The kingdom of God is not coming with signs to be observed; nor will they say, "Lo, here it is!" or "There!" for behold, the kingdom of God is in the midst of you.' (Luke 17:20-21). There is a real presence of the kingdom already now, but it is hidden. The hidden presence now and the glory to be manifest in the future are of course expressed in the parables concerning the seed and the final harvest.

The message and the reality of the kingdom is a 'treasure'. 'The kingdom of heaven is like treasure hidden in a field, which a man found and covered up; then in his joy he goes and sells all that he has and buys that field.' (Matt. 13:44). The treasure is not visible to everyone. But to the one who has discovered it, the kingdom is worth everything. The discovery of the treasure is the revelation that Jesus is the Messiah-King. His glory, his true identity, is hidden. In this age, it can only be known by faith. But in the age to come, it will be fully revealed, when 'the Son of man comes in his glory' (Matt. 25:31). For those who have found the 'treasure' there can be no turning back. 'No one who puts his hand to the plough and looks back is fit for the kingdom of God' (Luke 9:62).

With the first coming of Jesus, the kingdom was made present in hidden form. But at his second coming in glory, his *parousia*, the kingdom will be revealed and made fully manifest. Near the end of his Gospel account Luke tells us how Jesus responded to those who 'supposed that the kingdom of God was to appear immediately' (Luke 19:11). He tells the disciples a parable about 'a nobleman [who] went into a far country to receive a kingdom and then return' (19:12). The implication is that the nobleman will be away for some time. In his version of this parable Matthew makes this explicit: it was 'after a long time' that the master returned (Matt. 25:19).

The Kingdom and Righteousness

For Jesus, the kingdom of God establishes the righteousness of God. So in the Sermon on the Mount Jesus proclaims: 'Blessed are those who are persecuted for righteousness' sake, for theirs is the kingdom of heaven' (Matt. 5:10). In the next chapter, Jesus exhorts his disciples: 'seek first his kingdom and his righteousness, and all these things shall be yours as well' (Matt. 6:33).[3]

Righteousness was deeply embedded in the Jewish concept of God. In the prophetic writings, the denunciations of Israel and the promises of the coming messianic age give prominence to righteousness. The lack of righteousness in Israel is denounced,[4] and the fullness of righteousness in the coming age is promised. The prophet Isaiah says about the coming Davidic kingdom that the Lord 'will uphold it with justice and with righteousness from this time forth and for evermore' (Is. 9:7).[5] This righteousness is not just personal and private. It means the whole ordering of human relations and society, first in Israel, then in the Church and in the kingdom.

Righteousness (from the Hebrew root *sdq*) embraces both the inner dimension and a socially-embodied expression. It means godly order that is deeply rooted in those who are righteous. It is often used of the future of Jerusalem, as for example: 'The Lord bless you, O habitation of righteousness, O holy hill!' (Jer. 31:23). 'I will bring them to dwell in the midst of Jerusalem; and they shall be my people and I will be their God, in faithfulness and righteousness' (Zech. 8:8).

The Scriptures present the heart of God to establish righteousness upon earth. There are several passages that speak of God searching the earth for righteousness, and not finding it. There is the story of Abraham's pleading with God for Sodom, but even with the force of Abraham's prayer, the minimum number of righteous cannot be found (Gen. 18:22-33). The psalmist laments: 'The Lord looks down from heaven upon the children of men, to see if there are any that act wisely, that seek after God. They have all gone astray, they are all alike corrupt; there is none that does good, no, not one' (Ps. 14:2-3).[6] The prophet Jeremiah is told: 'Run to and fro through the streets of Jerusalem, look and take note! Search her squares to see if you can find a man, one who does justice and seeks truth; that I may pardon her' (Jer. 5:1).

Ultimately the righteous man whom God seeks will only come with the promised Messiah. In this promise about the righteous One to come, we glimpse the full dimensions of the righteousness which the Lord is preparing: 'Behold, the days are coming, says the Lord, when I will raise up for David a righteous Branch, and he shall reign as king and deal wisely, and shall execute justice and righteousness in the land. In his days Judah will be saved, and Israel will dwell securely. And this is the name by which he will be called: "The Lord is our righteousness"' (Jer. 23:5-6).

In the vision of the last judgement in Matthew 25, the king speaks to 'those at his right hand, "Come, O blessed of my Father, inherit the kingdom prepared for you from the foundation of the world"' (25:34). These are 'the righteous' who enter into 'eternal life' (25:46). This idea of the Father's plan prepared from the foundation of the world is, as we

shall see, at the heart of mystery in the teaching of
Paul.

FROM GOSPEL INTO THE MYSTERY

To make the word of God fully known
(Col. 1:25)

During the period from the earthly ministry of Jesus until the completion of the New Testament, a time-span of several decades, the infant Church goes through major trials and experiences significant growth. The Church spreads out from its Jewish origins into the Gentile world, both within the Roman Empire (mostly westwards) and outside it (to the east). From the earliest times, there are outbreaks of persecution against the disciples: first against the Greek-speaking Jewish believers in Jerusalem, including the death of the first martyr, Stephen (Acts 7); a few years later, James, the brother of John, is the first of the twelve to be killed (Acts 12:2). Later the Emperor Claudius commands all the Jews to leave Rome; as a result there is a scattering of Jewish believers, including a married couple, Aquila and Priscilla (Acts 18:2).

The biggest upheaval in this period is the Jewish rebellion of the year 66 CE, which leads to the Roman recapture of Jerusalem and the destruction of the temple in the year 70 CE. Up to this point, the Jewish believers in Jesus had continued to worship in the synagogue and to take part in temple worship. Many from Jerusalem had fled to Pella on the other side of the Jordan following a prophecy warning of the coming destruction. In any case, the Jewish disciples were less inclined to support the rebellion against Rome than their fellow Jews in Judea - no doubt because of their faith in the Messiah, crucified and risen, and because of the emerging Christian teaching to obey the ruling authorities (Rom. 13:1-7; 1 Peter 2:13-14).

The Initial Impetus

From the beginning the Christian movement is associated with the word 'gospel',[1] meaning good news. Christianity is first of all the proclamation of an event, an amazing happening unheard of in human history. That event is the resurrection of Jesus from the dead. But from the start this good news includes another event that quickly followed: the event of Pentecost, the outpouring of the Holy Spirit upon the first disciples. Through the gift of the Spirit at Pentecost the disciples who had seen the risen Jesus understand the significance of his resurrection and are empowered to proclaim the good news.

The first disciples are Jews. They preach to their fellow Jews. They tell them: This Jesus, whom you crucified, God has raised from the dead.[2] It is an event with revolutionary implications. The message of the resurrection of Jesus from the dead is good news for all, first for Jews and then for Gentiles. Because Jesus is risen, a new life is possible. The message is always: Jesus is risen, therefore ...

The Good News of Salvation

The first fruit of the resurrection of Jesus is the forgiveness of sins. 'God exalted him [Jesus] at his right hand as Leader and Saviour, to give repentance to Israel and forgiveness of sins' (Acts 5:31).[3] Paul puts this very bluntly: 'If Christ has not been raised, your faith is futile and you are still in your sins' (1 Cor. 15:17). From the start the gospel is a message of salvation.[4]

To understand why the resurrection of Jesus means the forgiveness of sins, we need to go back to the origins of sin. The Scriptures depict in story form the fact of human rebellion against God. The first man and the first woman directly disobey the command of the Lord. They are placed in the Garden of Eden, which symbolizes the abundance and the beauty of God's creation. Only one thing is forbidden: they must not eat from the tree of the knowledge of good and evil, 'for in the day that you eat of it you shall die' (Gen. 2:17). This narrative brings out the extraordinary generosity of God: everything God has created is available for this talented creature formed in his own image. The one restriction represents the one boundary human beings cannot cross: they cannot usurp the place of God and deny his authority.

The narration of the creation and the fall in Genesis chapters 2 and 3 is a masterpiece of story-telling. It depicts the temptation to rebellion in a way with which we can easily identify. The serpent insinuates that God is not being fair. Putting off -

limits the tree of the knowledge of good and evil is misrepresented as self-serving, as though God is trying to deprive us of something we ought to have: so 'the serpent said to the woman, "You will not die." For God knows that when you eat of it your eyes will be opened, and you will be like God, knowing good and evil' (Gen. 3:4-5).

But Adam and Eve believe the insinuation of the serpent rather than the word of God. We prefer the lies of the enemy to the promise of the all-bountiful Creator. The result is death. 'In the sweat of your face you shall eat bread till you return to the ground, for out of it you were taken; you are dust, and to dust you shall return' (Gen. 3:19). Many centuries later, the apostle Paul reflects on this catastrophe: 'sin came into the world through one man and death through sin' (Rom. 5:12) and 'the wages of sin is death' (Rom. 6:23).

Jesus came into the world to save us from our sins. He came to undo all the damage resulting from the original rebellion. 'The reason the Son of God appeared was to destroy the works of the devil' (1 John 3:8). Because death was the final fruit of sin, the conquering of sin required the conquering of death. This is why the resurrection of Jesus is the

most wonderful news. Jesus has conquered death.
This is the sign that Jesus has dealt with sin.
Because Jesus has conquered death, our sins can be
forgiven.

The second fruit of the resurrection of Jesus is the
gift of the Holy Spirit. When those who heard
Peter's preaching on the Day of Pentecost 'were cut
to the heart', they were told to 'Repent, and be
baptized every one of you in the name of Jesus
Christ for the forgiveness of your sins; and you
shall receive the gift of the Holy Spirit' (Acts 2:38).
Because Jesus had risen in his human body and
had been filled with the glory of God, he was able to
pour out the Holy Spirit: 'he has poured out this
which you see and hear' (Acts 2:33).

Because Jesus is risen, he can pour into us the
eternal life of God. Because Jesus is risen, we can
be filled with the love and the power that is in
Christ Jesus. We see the effects of this gift in the
transformed behaviour of the disciples: 'they were
all filled with the Holy Spirit and spoke the word of
God with boldness' (Acts 4:31). The first martyr
Stephen 'filled with the Holy Spirit' sees 'the glory
of God, and Jesus standing at the right hand of
God' (Acts 7:55).

The Gospel of Jesus Christ, the Son of God

The gospel message soon came to embrace the whole life and teachings of Jesus of Nazareth. The twelve, who were to be witnesses of his resurrection from the dead, had also to have been witnesses of his ministry 'during all the time that the Lord Jesus went in and out among us beginning from the baptism of John until the day when he was taken up from us' (Acts 1:21-22). So when four accounts of the life of Jesus and his teaching are put together, they are called 'gospels'. Of these, the second begins with the heading: 'The beginning of the gospel of Jesus Christ, the Son of God' (Mark 1:1).

In particular, the saving message came to be expressed in terms of the sacrificial death of Jesus, 'who was put to death for our trespasses and raised for our justification' (Rom. 4:25). In 1 Corinthians, this has come to take on a credal form: 'that Christ died for our sins in accordance with the scriptures, that he was buried, that he was raised on the third day in accordance with the scriptures' (1 Cor. 15:3-4).

As the message of the resurrection spread out from the people of Israel to the Gentiles, the peoples of the nations, there is a new insistence on the moral transformation of the believer. We can see this in the first letter written by the apostle Paul, the first letter to the Thessalonians: 'For this is the will of God, your sanctification: that you abstain from unchastity ... For God has not called us for uncleanness, but in holiness' (1 Thess. 4:3,7). Paul upbraids the Corinthians: 'Do you not know that the unrighteous will not inherit the kingdom of God? Do not be deceived; neither the immoral, nor idolaters, nor adulterers, nor sexual perverts, nor thieves, nor the greedy, nor drunkards, nor revilers, nor robbers will inherit the kingdom of God' (1 Cor. 6:9-10).

As Jews, the first disciples had believed in the coming of the Messiah, the Son of David, who would reign on the throne of Israel and deliver his people from Gentile oppression. But Jesus, whom they had confessed to be the Christ, was put to death. We catch the depth of disappointed hopes from the reluctance of the disciples to believe in his resurrection: 'but these words seemed to them an idle tale, and they did not believe them' (Luke 24:11).

After Pentecost, the disciples understood that Jesus had been enthroned as Messiah at the right hand of the Father, but not yet in Jerusalem. The hope of Israel is not switched from earth to heaven, but from the first coming of the Messiah as a servant to his second coming in glory on the clouds of heaven. We can see this transposition in Peter's homily in Acts 3, where he says that the prophecies that the Messiah would suffer have been fulfilled (3:18), but that the full restoration promised in the Old Testament is yet to be accomplished when the Messiah comes again: 'Repent therefore, and turn again, that your sins may be blotted out, that times of refreshing may come from the presence of the Lord, and that he may send the Christ [Messiah] appointed for you, Jesus, whom heaven must receive until the time for establishing all that God spoke by the mouth of his holy prophets from of old' (3:19-21).

This hope of the second coming of Jesus and of the full establishing of the kingdom of God is preached throughout the New Testament, repeated perhaps more than any other doctrine. And almost as frequently, the New Testament authors insist that in the meantime, Christians are to live holy lives, without reproach: Christians are to love one another and all people 'so that he [the Lord] may establish your hearts unblamable in holiness before our God and Father, at the coming of our Lord Jesus with all his saints' (1 Thess. 3:13). 'I charge you to keep the commandment unstained and free from reproach until the appearing of our Lord Jesus Christ' (1 Tim. 6:14).[5]

Summary: The good news preached by the apostles from the Day of Pentecost is first the proclamation of the event of Jesus' resurrection. It includes all that the resurrection made possible: first, the forgiveness of sins and the gift of the Holy Spirit. This new life in the Spirit involves a transformation from the old ways of the flesh to the love, joy and peace of the gospel. The Christian is a 'new creation': 'Therefore, if anyone is in Christ, he is a new creation; the old has passed away, behold, the new has come' (2 Cor. 5:17). All that flows from the good news of the resurrection is then ordered towards the second coming of Jesus and the fullness of the kingdom. Even now the Christian tastes the first fruits of the age to come.

According to God's Purpose

From the beginnings of the Church, the apostles understand the resurrection of Jesus and the outpouring of the Holy Spirit as fulfilling the promises of the Lord. Jesus had been 'delivered up according to the definite plan and foreknowledge of God' (Acts 2:23). 'And all the prophets who have spoken, from Samuel and those who came afterwards, also proclaimed these days' (Acts 3:24). In Galatians, Paul says of our Lord Jesus Christ that he 'gave himself for our sins to deliver us from the present evil age, according to the will of our God and Father' (Gal. 1:4).

This Christian conviction that the Jesus-event was ordained by God reflects the long-standing Jewish belief in the one God, who is at the same time the God of Abraham, Isaac and Jacob, and the creator of the whole cosmos. 'Thus says the Lord, the King of Israel and his Redeemer, the Lord of hosts: "I am the first and I am the last; besides me, there is no god. Who is like me? Let him proclaim it, let him declare and set it forth before me. Who has announced from of old the things to come?"' (Is. 44:6-7).

The Jewish doctrine of creation means that everything has a purpose. The God who created all things out of nothing could not toy with the world. The first creation story of the seven days of creation is deeply purposeful, building up to the crescendo, the creation of man and woman, deputed to take care of the world in all its beauty and richness. It is the apostle Paul who deepens the Church's understanding of God's eternal plan, no doubt aided by his rabbinical training. The Christian message is not just the gospel of salvation; it is the unfolding of the eternal plan of the Father.

Paul's Idea of Mystery

As Paul comes to understand more deeply the plan of God in the light of the resurrection of Jesus he begins to use the word 'mystery'. The term is not used in his first letters, the two letters to the Thessalonians, except in reference to 'the mystery of iniquity' (2 Thess. 2:7).[6]

For Paul, 'mystery' sums up the whole purpose of God. Mystery means the eternal plan of God: the plan of God in all creation, the plan of God in the call of Israel, the plan of God in the sending of his Son to save and redeem, the plan of God for the kingdom founded in Jesus and to be fully established at his return in glory. There are four passages in particular which present the key elements in Paul's concept of mystery: Rom. 16:25-26; Eph. 1:9-10; 3:4-6; Col. 1:26.

Hidden From All Ages

God has had this plan from all eternity. It has always been God's purpose, if we can use a time-bound word like 'always' to express what simply is in God.

However, God's plan had been hidden. Nobody had known it. It remained in the heart of the Father. It governed God's actions. God's plan or purpose 'was kept secret for long ages' (Rom. 16:25). It 'was not made known to the sons of men in other generations' (Eph. 3:5). It was 'the mystery hidden for ages and generations' (Col. 1:26).

In another passage, Paul says that he speaks 'God's wisdom in mystery that has been hidden' (1 Cor. 2:7). This was decreed by God 'before the ages for our glorification'. Before time began, God had this wonderful plan for the creation that he will bring into being. This is also the perspective of the

opening verses of Ephesians, the letter that has the
most references to 'the mystery'. 'Blessed be the
God and Father of our Lord Jesus Christ, who has
blessed us in Christ with every spiritual blessing in
the heavenly places, even as he chose us in him
before the foundation of the world, that we should
be holy and blameless before him' (Eph. 1:3-4).

While it is hard for us to imagine what this eternal
choice means, it is clear that nothing is an after-
thought for God. We were present in the mind of
God before we came into being, indeed before
anyone came into being. We had an extraordinary
destiny marked out for us, even before there was
sin and rebellion among the angels or on the earth.

In the book of Proverbs, we read: 'It is the glory of
God to conceal things, but the glory of kings is to
search things out' (25:2). We do well to ponder the
depth and wisdom of this statement. We might
think that God loves to reveal and to show forth his
majesty. But in our human experience, we know
that the things that are dearest to our hearts we do
not easily share. We share the deepest things only
with those who are most dear to us. But the things
of God are the deepest things of all. It is God's
wisdom to hide. It is his glory to conceal. But God

is not like one who hoards hidden treasure. The hiddenness is not for ever, and it is for a purpose.

For the Fullness of Time

This holy purpose of God remained hidden for long ages and generations. This speaks to us of its preciousness and depth. God longed to make his plan known. But what God has kept hidden is so holy, so deep, so magnificent, that it cannot be casually shown forth. In his great wisdom, God knew that a long preparation was needed before he unveiled the secret of his heart. The mystery is 'a plan for the fullness of time' (Eph. 1:10).

At the heart of this preparation was the choice of a people. God chose a people to be his own, the people of Israel, a people he could train and prepare for the unveiling of his secret. So Paul compares the time of preparation for this unveiling to childhood awaiting and preparing for adult maturity. 'I mean that the heir, as long as he is a child, is no better than a slave, though he is the owner of all the estate; but he is under guardians and trustees until the date set by the father' (Gal. 4:1-2).

Set Forth in Christ

The plan of God that is the mystery 'hidden from all
ages' is now 'set forth in Christ' (Eph. 1:9). The
long centuries of hiddenness are over with the
appearing of God's Son. The secrets of the Father's
heart are made accessible in the heart of his
incarnate Son. It is not an end to all hiddenness,
for in Christ 'are hid all the treasures of wisdom
and knowledge' (Col. 2:3). The unveiling of the
mystery is an unveiling to faith, and it is the work
of the Holy Spirit.[7]

This plan which centres on Jesus is God's purpose
for all creation. Jesus is 'the first-born of all
creation' (Col. 1:15) and 'the first-born from the
dead' (Col. 1:18). The eternal Son has first place in
God's plan in creation, and in his resurrection he is
first in the new creation: so Paul speaks of Jesus as
'the last Adam' (1 Cor. 15:45). In the eyes of the
Father, everything is related to his Son. In fact,
Paul even says: 'all things were created through
him and for him. He is before all things, and in
him all things hold together' (Col. 1:16-17).

We can now turn to the revelation of the mystery of
Messiah: the revelation of his coming in the flesh

(Chapter 3), the revelation of his mission and ministry (Chapter 4) and the deeper revelation of his person (Chapter 5).

Part II

The Mystery of Christ

HE WAS MANIFESTED
IN THE FLESH

*Great indeed is the mystery of our religion
(1 Tim. 3:16)*

Paul tells us clearly: the mystery is Jesus the
Christ. He speaks of 'the knowledge of God's
mystery, of Christ' (Col. 2:2). He refers to 'the
mystery of Christ' (Eph. 3:4; Col. 4:3). The treasure
hidden from all ages is God's Son. This is the
secret God reveals in the fullness of time: 'I have a
son.'

Remember the parables of Jesus that speak of the
king's son. 'Afterward he sent his son to them,
saying, "They will respect my son"' (Matt. 21:37).
'The kingdom of heaven may be compared to a king
who gave a marriage feast for his son' (Matt. 22:2).
God sends his Son to the rebellious tenants of the
vineyard. The king brings forth his Son before his
people.

Thus, at the heart of God's plan is a person. The mystery is not a system or a timetable. At its heart it concerns the beloved of the Father, his only-begotten Son. So at two special moments in the life of Jesus, at his baptism in the Jordan and at his transfiguration on the mountain, a voice is heard from heaven declaring: 'This is my Son, with whom I am well pleased' (Matt. 3:17; 17:5).

Manifested in the Flesh

With the coming of Christ, the Messiah of Israel, the Son of God, God's eternal purpose is made known. In fact, God's purpose is not just made known, it is made human flesh. 'The Word became flesh and dwelt among us, full of grace and truth' (John 1:14). In Jesus of Nazareth, the heart of God is made visible. 'That which was from the beginning, which we have heard, which we have seen with our eyes, which we have looked upon and touched with our hands, concerning the word of life - the life was made manifest, and we saw it, and testify to it, and proclaim to you the eternal life which was with the Father and was made manifest to us' (1 John 1:1-2).

Paul expresses this in his first letter to Timothy:
'Great indeed, we confess, is the mystery of our
religion: He was manifested in the flesh, vindicated
in the Spirit, seen by angels, preached among the
nations, believed on in the world, taken up in glory'
(1 Tim. 3:16). Since this is expressed in verse form
as poetry, Paul may be citing a hymn already used
in the Church. This view is confirmed by the
primitive character of the language, particularly
the phrase 'vindicated in the Spirit' to refer to the
resurrection of Jesus. This verse shows that the
mystery is not just the Son of God coming in the
flesh, but embraces his whole life and its
consummation in ascension to glory.

The fullness of time is the chosen time for the
incarnation. 'When the time had fully come, God
sent forth his Son, born of woman, born under the
law' (Gal. 4:4). The centuries of preparation have
passed. The people of Israel have been schooled
through the ages in monotheism, faith in the one
and only God of their fathers, who is also the
creator of all things. A deep abhorrence for idolatry
has been imprinted in the Jewish mind. Without
such a training, the revelation of God's only Son
could never be understood correctly.

Like Us in All Things except Sin

In the incarnation, the Son of God became truly and fully human. Jesus begins his life like any other baby in the womb of his mother. Though not conceived by human means, but by the power of the Holy Spirit (Matt. 1:20), the child so conceived is formed and grows normally in his mother's womb; he is born, he passes through the normal phases of infancy, childhood and growth to manhood. Jesus cries as a baby. He suffers the pains of teething when his first teeth come through. He stumbles when he first tries to walk. He learns from Joseph and Mary as any child learns from its parents. He makes friends in Nazareth as other children make friends where they live. Jesus is like us in every way with one exception. The only difference is that Jesus is without sin.

Being without sin is of course a huge difference. Sin is not a minimal factor! This might lead us to think that Jesus isn't really like us at all. However, the New Testament makes a point of telling us that Jesus is tempted, and does so in the precise passage that speaks of him being without sin. 'For we have not a high priest who is unable to sympathise with our weaknesses, but one who in every respect has been tempted as we are, yet without sin' (Heb. 4:15). The Greek translated as 'in every respect' is *katà pánta*, meaning literally 'in all (things)'. Jesus is subjected to all the temptations to which human beings are subject. But he does not give way.

There is one other passage in Hebrews that speaks of Jesus becoming like us in every way (again *katà pánta*): 'Therefore he had to be made like his brethren in every respect, so that he might become a merciful and faithful high priest in the service of God, to make expiation for the sins of the people' (Heb. 2:17). The author makes it very clear that this enfleshment of Jesus is for our sakes, for us who are weak and sinful. 'For because he himself has suffered and been tempted, he is able to help those who are tempted' (Heb. 2:18).

The phrase 'in the flesh' emphasizes that Jesus fully shares our human condition in this suffering world. This is dramatically expressed in the prologue to John's Gospel. John speaks of 'the Word' who 'was with God, and the Word was God' (John 1:1). It is of this eternal divine Word that he then says: 'And the Word became flesh and dwelt among us, full of grace and truth' (John 1:14). The Greek word translated as 'flesh' is *sàrx*. To say that the Word became *sàrx* is more than saying that God took on a human body. There is another Greek word for body (*sōma*). *Sàrx* conveys the sense of human weakness, that Jesus entered into the condition of suffering humanity. So the statement that he became *sàrx*, that he became flesh, has a dramatic quality.

Suffered in the Flesh

Because he is truly human, and takes on real human flesh, Jesus can suffer and die. The most explicit reflection on his 'suffering in the flesh' is also in Hebrews. 'In the days of his flesh, Jesus offered up prayers and supplications, with loud cries and tears, to him who was able to save him from death, and he was heard for his godly fear' (Heb. 5:7). This seems to be a reference to the prayer of Jesus in the garden of Gethsemane. The phrase 'with loud cries and tears' points to the depth of the agony in the heart of Jesus as he faced the desertion of his disciples and the prospect of a brutal execution. It unveils a little more of what Matthew reports of Jesus in his agony: 'My soul is very sorrowful, even to death' (Matt. 26:38). That

Jesus suffers 'in the flesh' means that his total humanity is involved - in every respect. Indeed, because he is without sin, he suffers more acutely than all others who are less sensitive. Jesus is so humanly sensitive to all that is happening around him that he suffers intensely in his soul 'even to death'.

The agony of Jesus is fully human. In his passion, he suffers in every part of his being - in his body, in his emotions, in his affections, in his soul. On the cross, Jesus cites a verse from Psalm 22, so the whole psalm must have been in his mind: 'I am poured out like water, and all my bones are out of joint; my heart is like wax, it is melted within my breast; my strength is dried up like a potsherd, and my tongue cleaves to my jaws' (Ps. 22:14-15).

Through the passion of Jesus, the salvation of God is wrought in human flesh. The flesh of Jesus is the battlefield where the enemy throws in every weapon to defeat the citadel of righteousness. The fiercest temptation of Jesus is on the cross. This is the 'opportune time' when the devil resumes his attack on Jesus (see Luke 4:13). Paul describes this battle: 'For God has done what the law, weakened by the flesh, could not do: sending his own Son in the likeness of sinful flesh and for sin, he condemned sin in the flesh' (Rom. 8:3).

The temptation of Jesus on the cross is most clearly brought out in 1 Pet. 2: 'He committed no sin; no guile was found on his lips. When he was reviled, he did not revile in return; when he suffered, he did not threaten; but he trusted to him who judges justly' (vv.22-23). Jesus resists totally everything in human nature that wants to bad-mouth the critic and to destroy the assailant. He refuses to judge and places all in the hands of his Father. 'He himself bore our sins in his body on the tree, that we might die to sin and live to righteousness. By his wounds you have been healed' (v.24). Because Jesus in no way yields to the tempter, he cannot be held by the bonds of death. 'But God raised him up, having loosed the pangs of death, because it was not possible for him to be held by it' (Acts 2:24).

The significance of Jesus suffering 'in the flesh' is enhanced by the fact that even after his resurrection, his body still bears the marks of Calvary. This is shown not only in the episode with 'doubting' Thomas, who is invited to place his hand in the wounded side of Jesus (John 20:27), but also in the vision of John in the book of Revelation.

John sees 'a Lamb standing, as though it had been slain' (Rev. 5:6). The marks of crucifixion remain.

Bodily Resurrection

The heart of the good news is that on the third day after his death on the cross, Jesus rose in the body. The reality of the risen body of Jesus is made clear in some of his resurrection appearances. It is evident in the invitation to Thomas. It is brought out explicitly in an episode reported by Luke. As some of the disciples saw the risen Jesus appear among them, 'they were startled and frightened, and supposed that they saw a spirit' (Luke 24:37). Jesus gives a direct answer to show that he is not just a ghost or a spirit: 'Why are you troubled, and why do questionings rise in your hearts? See my hands and my feet, that it is I myself; handle me, and see; for a spirit has not flesh and bones as you see that I have' (Luke 24:38-39).

The resurrection appearances of Jesus are not revelations of a dazzling glory like the transfiguration or the vision of Jesus in Revelation.[1] The Gospel of John, which is particularly attentive to the glory of Jesus, has the story of Jesus and Mary Magdalene, in which he tells her, 'Do not hold me, for I have not yet ascended to the Father' (John 20:17). The full glorification of Jesus occurs in his ascension to the Father. This is when his humanity is totally filled and penetrated with the glory of God. As the total filling with the Holy Spirit, this represents the 'spiritualizing' of the body, and is the final destiny for which God has created us humans.[2]

This is no doubt why Paul speaks in 1 Cor. 15 of the resurrected body as a 'spiritual body' (*sōma pneumatikón*): 'It is sown a physical body, it is raised a spiritual body' (1 Cor. 15:44). The adjective 'spiritual' refers to a quality; it indicates the kind of body we will have after the resurrection. It does not mean that it is not a body any more. Rather the body is now ruled by the spirit, indwelled by the Holy Spirit of God, no longer under the domination of the psychic or the physical.

Born a Jew

The Christian doctrine of the incarnation is not just that God's only Son took on human flesh. The Son of God entered human history at a particular place and a particular time. Jesus is not just born to a human mother, but he is born to a particular woman, Mary of Nazareth. Mary belongs to a particular tribe and a particular people. She belongs to the tribe of Judah of the people of Israel. So Jesus enters into this heritage. He has human ancestors. Matthew begins his Gospel with the words: 'The book of the genealogy of Jesus Christ, the son of David, the son of Abraham' (Matt. 1:1).

There are days in the Church's liturgy when the full genealogy of the ancestors of Jesus is read out, whether from Matthew (Matt. 1:2-16) or from Luke (Luke 3:23-38). It may not be very inspiring to hear a long succession of 'A was the father of B, B the father of C, C the father of D'. But there is a deep wisdom in the choice of these passages. They protect us from viewing the incarnation as a magical intervention. Matthew, who traces the line from Abraham through David down to Joseph, is focused on the fulfilment of the promise, first made to Abraham concerning his 'seed'. Luke works back from Joseph through David and Abraham to Adam. Matthew has the Jewish focus that Jesus possesses the Jewish inheritance of the son of Abraham according to the promise. Luke has the Gentile emphasis, that sees the universal significance of Jesus, as descendant of Adam, thus reinforcing the universal import of the call of the sons of Abraham to be a blessing to all nations.

Manifested in Jewish Flesh

Jesus is born a Jew. He is born into the family of Joseph and Mary. They are devout Jews of the tribe of Judah. They observe the requirements of the Law of Moses. On the eighth day, the infant son born to Mary is circumcised and given the name Jesus that she had been given by the angel (Luke 2:21;1:31). The name Jesus was a typically Jewish name, a name that expressed a characteristic activity of the God of Israel: in this case, God saves. It is the same name as Joshua the Israelite leader after Moses, as well as the name borne by the author of the book of Ecclesiasticus, also known as Sirach.

The parents of Jesus observe the laws of purification, so that after forty days they bring the baby Jesus up to Jerusalem to 'present him to the Lord' (Luke 2:22). The episode when Jesus is twelve years old, when Mary and Joseph find him discussing with the teachers in the temple, hints at his official coming of age in the Jewish community. This celebration of bar-mitzvah at the age of thirteen must have shortly followed for Jesus at Nazareth, though in his day the celebrations were not as elaborate as they later became in Jewish tradition. Everything about the comportment of Mary and Joseph that we learn from the Gospels points to Jesus receiving a very thorough grounding in the life and spirituality of his people.

The incarnation of God's Son confirms a fundamental principle in God's dealings with his creation. God chooses a particular person in order to bless all. God chose Abraham so that in him 'all the families of the earth shall bless themselves' (Gen. 12:3). Israel is called to be a priestly people among the peoples of the earth, all of whom belong to God. So God says to Moses, 'Now therefore, if you will obey my voice and keep my covenant, you shall be my own possession among all peoples; for all the earth is mine, and you shall be to me a kingdom of priests and a holy nation' (Ex. 19:5-6). David was chosen from the tribe of Judah to be king over all Israel. 'Once for all I have sworn by my holiness; I will not lie to David. His line shall endure for ever, his throne as long as the sun before me' (Ps. 89:35-36). The suffering servant of Yahweh in Isaiah is another figure who represents his whole people: 'I have given you as a covenant to the people' (Is. 42:6).

This principle is also true of Mary. She is chosen out of the tribe of Judah to play a representative role in Israel as mother of the Messiah. The authentic Christian veneration of Mary is grounded in the profound reality of the incarnation: all that is involved in the eternal Word taking on human flesh from a young Jewish woman. God never treats humans as mere impersonal instruments. Mary is not to be seen as a divine incubator, needed only to bring a baby into the world. She is the Israelite chosen to embody the maternal role of Israel in bringing the Messiah into the world. Her role is not exhausted by the upbringing of the child, but extends to the marriage feast at Cana (John 2:1-11), to the foot of the cross (John 19:25-27) and to the birth of the Church (Acts 1:14).

Jesus is the chosen one of God. He is son of Abraham, son of David. He is the suffering servant, who embodies the priestly suffering call of Israel. In all these ways, he is the instrument of the Father to bless all peoples and all nations - precisely through total fidelity to his calling as son of Abraham and son of David.

RECONCILING THE WORLD TO HIMSELF

To unite all things in him, things in
heaven and things on earth (Eph. 1:10)

As we have seen, the word 'mystery' opens up the
vista of the plan of God for the entire creation.
This plan has Jesus as its centre. In the last
chapter, we looked at the life of Jesus, and how his
coming in the flesh was lived out from his
conception and birth through to his glorious
ascension. Now we turn to the mission of Jesus, to
the role that Jesus plays in the execution and
fulfilment of God's eternal plan.

In Eph.1 Paul expresses clearly the role that Jesus
Christ, the Son of God, plays in relation to the
whole of God's creation. God has a plan for
everything and everyone that he has made. All is
to be brought into harmony and unity through
Jesus and in relation to him. 'For he has made

known to us in all wisdom and insight the mystery of his will, according to his purpose which he set forth in Christ as a plan for the fullness of time, to unite all things in him, things in heaven and things on earth' (Eph. 1:9-10).

The Effects of Sin

The Scriptures tell the story of salvation and redemption. They speak of the original creation, of humankind's fall from grace and descent into sin, and then of the rescue work of God, the gradual unfolding of a remarkable plan of healing and restoration. To grasp the magnitude of salvation, we must understand the devastation wrought by sin.

Sin is rebellion against God. Sin rejects God's authority. God's authority is the principle of order. All created things find their rightful place within God's order as they come under his authority. Sin produces disorder. Sin leads to chaos.

Sin is a refusal of God's love. Love affirms and respects others. 'Love is patient and kind; love is not jealous or boastful; it is not arrogant or rude. Love does not insist on its own way; it is not irritable or resentful' (1 Cor. 13:4-5). Sin finds many ways to destroy authentic love. It destroys love by love's opposite that is hatred. It destroys love by the distortion of lustful desire that may feel like love, but is never far from hatred, as we see in the story of David's son, Amnon, who raped his half-sister Tamar. 'Then Amnon hated her with very great hatred; so that the hatred with which he hated her was greater than the love with which he had loved her' (2 Sam. 13:15). Sin undermines love by fear and suspicion.

Sin violates community and communion. For individuals, sin easily leads to isolation and separation. Self-indulgence produces a self-absorption that weakens and destroys relationships. In groups and communities, sin provokes division. Notice strife, dissension and party spirit in Paul's list of the works of the flesh (Gal. 5:20).

Sin violates God's truth. Jesus says of Satan: 'When he lies, he speaks according to his own nature, for he is a liar and the father of lies' (John 8:44). In the original temptation presented in Genesis 3, the serpent denies the word of God, who had said, 'You shall not eat of the fruit of the tree

which is in the midst of the garden, neither shall
you touch it, lest you die' (Gen. 3:3). 'But the
serpent said to the woman, "You will not die"'(Gen.
3:4). When we sin, we believe a lie. We believe the
lie of the enemy that says, 'Do what you want. God
is out to deprive you of enjoyment and fulfilment.
You will only be happy and free if you can do what
you want.' The first sin then leads to lies and
deception. Saul is disobedient to the Lord, and
then lies to Samuel (1 Sam. 15:13-14). David
commits adultery with Bathsheba and is deceitful
with Uriah (2 Sam. 11). Ananias and Sapphira
hold back part of the proceeds of the land they have
sold and pretend they are giving the whole. Peter
speaks of their 'lie to the Holy Spirit' (Acts 5:3).
Lying and deception destroy human communication. They poison the atmosphere and render
understanding more difficult.

The end-product of sin is death. Death entered the
world through sin 'and so death spread to all men
because all men sinned' (Rom. 5:12). 'For the wages
of sin is death' (Rom. 6:23). Death is the ultimate
consequence of sin. Death is human disintegration,
the departure of life from the body which then
dissolves into dust. The disintegration that we see

in the tormented lives of drug addicts, alcoholics, serial adulterers, power-hungry tyrants is a horrifying picture of the disintegration that results from all sin.

First Steps to Redemption

God's chosen way of rescuing the human race from its addiction to sin is to form a particular people to whom he will teach his ways and through whom he will bring the Saviour into the world. As sin has scattered, so salvation gathers and restores. In the history of the people of Israel, chosen to be God's own possession, we find many signs of God's redeeming purpose:

- God leads his people out of the slavery of Egypt on a journey to the Promised Land; this journey is later understood as a type or picture of the process leading from the slavery of sin to the bounty of heaven.

- On this journey, God gives his people the ten commandments (Ex. 20:3-17; Deut. 5:7-21) and structures the life of this people he has gathered to be his own.

- God prescribes sacrifices for different kinds of sin (Lev. 1-7).

- The people are given the Day of Atonement (Yom Kippur) as a special day each year for the confession of the people's sin and the offering of sacrifice by the high priest in the most holy place (Lev. 16; 23:27-32).

- The thrice-yearly pilgrimages to Jerusalem are a sign of God's future ingathering of his people in his holy city. 'Jerusalem, built as a city, which is bound firmly together, to which the tribes go up, the tribes of the Lord, as was decreed for Israel' (Ps. 122:3-4).

Israel's Sin Leads to Exile

The people of Israel, to whom are given the law, the land, the city and the temple, are themselves disobedient to the Lord. The time of the judges is a period of constant backsliding and regular recall to the Lord. Hardly is the kingdom established in Jerusalem under David than the king sins grievously and introduces strife into his own family. Through the prophet Nathan, the Lord says to David: 'Now therefore the sword shall never depart from your house' (2 Sam. 12:10). The sin of David is forgiven, but he must live with its consequences, including the violent death of three of his sons.

Solomon's sin leads to the division of the kingdom after his death. In this episode, we see how the Lord visits upon his people the consequences of Solomon's infidelity while remaining faithful to his promises to David: 'Therefore the Lord said to Solomon, "Since this has been your mind and you have not kept my covenant and my statutes which I have commanded you, I will surely tear the kingdom from you and will give it to your servant. Yet for the sake of David your father I will not do it in your days, but I will tear it out of the hand of your son. However I will not tear away all the kingdom; but I will give one tribe to your son, for the sake of David my servant and for the sake of Jerusalem which I have chosen"' (1 Kings 11:11-13).

After the division of the kingdom, the northern kingdom is constantly unfaithful, dynasties regularly replace one another, and finally in 722 BCE. the kingdom is destroyed and the people are dispersed. The history of the southern kingdom, the kingdom of Judah, is not much better. Here, however, there are occasionally righteous kings, such as Asa, Hezekiah and Josiah. But in the end, the prophets denounce Judah as worse than the vanished northern kingdom of Israel (see Ez. 23:11).

The result is an unimaginable disaster. The temple is destroyed. The holy city is devastated. Many are taken into exile in Babylon. The Jews see before their eyes the consequences of their sin. The agony of the faithful Jew, who loved the Lord and his heritage, is poignantly expressed in the book of Lamentations: 'Jerusalem sinned grievously, therefore she became filthy; all who honoured her despised her, for they have seen her nakedness; yea, she herself groans, and turns her face away. Her uncleanness was in her skirts; she took no thought of her doom; therefore her fall is terrible, she has no comforter. "O Lord, behold my affliction, for the enemy has triumphed!"' (Lam. 1:8-9).

Promises of Return and Ingathering

Amazingly, in the midst of catastrophe following Israel's constant disobedience, the Lord promises a wonderful restoration for his people. The exiles will be gathered from all the corners of the earth to which they have been scattered. The Lord will

raise an ensign or a standard as a sign for the great
return. In Is. 11, it is the root of Jesse whom the
nations seek (v.10): 'He will raise an ensign for the
nations, and will assemble the outcasts of Israel,
and gather the dispersed of Judah from the four
corners of the earth' (Is. 11:12).[1] Through the
prophet Jeremiah, the Lord promises: 'Behold, I
will bring them from the north country, and gather
them from the farthest parts of the earth' (Jer.
31:8).[2] God will pour out the Spirit to create a new
heart in his people able and willing to live in
fellowship with him.[3] In this future vision the
nations of the earth streaming to Israel are
sometimes doomed to judgment[4] and sometimes
destined for blessing. Of Jerusalem, it is said: 'all
the nations shall flow to it, and many peoples shall
come, and say, 'Come, let us go up to the mountain
of the Lord, to the house of the God of Jacob; that
he may teach us his ways and that we may walk in
his paths' (Is. 2:2-3).[5]

These promises of salvation and ingathering are to
be fulfilled by the Messiah, Son of David. It is
Jesus of Nazareth who will save and gather in his
people, and who will save and gather in the nations
of the earth.

Jesus Saves and Gathers

Throughout his life Jesus lives totally for the glory of the Father. This fidelity and obedience is the necessary framework for the fulfilment of his mission. At the outset of his public ministry, the obedience of Jesus is severely tested in the three temptations in the wilderness.

Immediately after the temptations in the wilderness, Jesus begins to preach the kingdom of God and to gather disciples to be trained in the way of the kingdom. In the Sermon on the Mount, Jesus gives them the Beatitudes, which sum up the lifestyle and the values of the coming kingdom. Here is a stark antithesis to the ways of the world which boost the ego, place self-interest first, regard riches as security and mercy as weakness. The Beatitudes express the life-style of Jesus: he hungers and thirsts for righteousness, he is merciful, he is pure in heart, he is a peacemaker, he is persecuted for righteousness' sake.[6]

Jesus ministers to the crowds who follow him, and to the individuals who seek him out. But always there is the formation of the disciples who accompany him wherever he goes. There is preaching to the crowds, and there is teaching for the disciples. In particular, Jesus chooses twelve men to be the core leadership of the community of those who accept his message and the salvation he will bring. Among these disciples, chief place is given to Simon Peter, the first to confess Jesus as the Messiah and the Son of the living God.

It is to Peter that Jesus first speaks of the Church. 'And I tell you, you are Peter and on this rock I will build my church, and the powers of death shall not prevail against it' (Matt. 16:18). Though the Greek word *ekklēsia*, here translated as church, meant a political gathering in the Greek world, in the Greek translation of the Old Testament, it translated the Hebrew word *qahal*. *Qahal* was the word used to describe the assembly of Israel at Mount Horeb (Deut. 4:10), in Moab before the crossing into the Promised Land (Deut. 31:30), at Mount Ebal (Jos. 8:35) and with King David in Jerusalem (1 Chron. 28:8). The word 'church' appears again in Matthew 18:17. In this passage Jesus speaks of his presence with the disciples who gather in his name: 'For where two or three are gathered in my name, there am I in the midst of them' (Matt. 18:20).

Ironically, the most important and solemn gathering of the twelve comes immediately before one of them betrays Jesus and the rest are scattered. This is on the occasion of the Last Supper, when Jesus says to the twelve: 'I have earnestly desired to eat this passover with you before I suffer; for I tell you I shall not eat it until it is fulfilled in the kingdom of God' (Luke 22:15-16). The Passover is the Jewish feast that celebrates their origins as a people with the exodus from Egypt. It is at this moment that Jesus establishes the Eucharist as the gathering of his disciples who will obey his command to take bread and wine and to 'Do this in remembrance of me' (Luke 22:19). For the time of the Church from Pentecost to the second coming, the disciples will gather to celebrate the Pasch of the Lord Jesus: 'Thus from celebration to celebration, as they proclaim the Paschal mystery of Jesus "until he comes," the pilgrim People of God advances, "following the narrow way of the cross," towards the heavenly banquet, when all the elect will be seated at the table of the kingdom.'[7]

The Ingathering through the Church

The age of the Church begins on the Day of Pentecost with the outpouring of the Holy Spirit from the risen, ascended Jesus. Church (*ekklēsia*) means those 'called out of'. The Church is the body of those called out of sin and brought into the assembly of the holy God. But the Church also becomes the instrument through which the kingdom of God is announced, and others are brought into the assembled family of God. The plan of God is to bring back into unity all the peoples of the earth. So the last words of Jesus before his ascension are a command to witness to his saving work throughout the earth: 'you shall be my witnesses in Jerusalem and in all Judea and Samaria and to the end of the earth' (Acts 1:8). Through the power of the Holy Spirit, the disciples are to gather into one body people from every subsequent age and generation in human history, people from every race and nation, and from every tribe and language. In the next chapter, we shall look more specifically at the special place of the Jewish people in this process.

In the missionary endeavours, the first priority of the disciples is to preach the gospel, the Word of God. 'Faith comes from what is heard, and what is heard comes by the preaching of Christ' (Rom. 10:17). The preaching leads to the re-birth of baptism through the coming together of the water and the Word. 'You have been born anew, not of perishable seed but of imperishable, through the living and abiding word of God' (1 Peter 1:23).

Those re-born in baptism are conformed to Christ and built into his unity through the celebration of the Eucharist. Indeed, Paul probably came to understand that the Church is the body of Christ through feeding on the body of Christ in the Eucharist. 'The bread which we break, is it not a participation in the body of Christ? Because there is one bread, we who are many are one body, for we all partake of the one bread' (1 Cor. 10:16-17). As we feed on the one body of the Lord, we are formed into one body, that is his body. The eucharistic banquet is a foretaste and sign of the banquet of the coming kingdom that Jesus promised his disciples.[8]

At the same time as the disciples are going out to proclaim the gospel of Jesus Christ to Israel and the nations, the Holy Spirit is leading them into a deeper understanding of the Father's purpose. This is the process from gospel into mystery. There is a realization of the cosmic scope of the salvific work of Jesus, and of his role as head of the Church that is his body. This cosmic vision is especially presented in Paul's letters to the Ephesians and the Colossians.

In Colossians, Paul places the ingathering of all things in the context of Christ's role in creation. In Christ 'all things were created, in heaven and on earth, visible and invisible ... all things were created through him and for him. He is before all things, and in him all things hold together' (Col. 1:15-17). So it is in Christ, 'that all the fullness of God was pleased to dwell, and through him to reconcile to himself all things, whether on earth or in heaven, making peace by the blood of his cross' (Col. 1:19-20). This saving and reconciling ministry of Jesus is established in his resurrection and ascension. Through the resurrection and ascension the fullness of God fills the humanity of Jesus and he enters fully into his ministry as universal Saviour and Lord of all.

Paul uses the image of the building of a temple to describe this process of reconciliation and reintegration. This building, established upon the foundation of the apostles and prophets, with Christ Jesus as the cornerstone, 'is joined together and grows into a holy temple in the Lord' (Eph. 2:21). Later in the same epistle, he speaks of the ministries established 'for building up the body of Christ' (Eph. 4:12). We, the Christians, 'are to grow up in every way into him who is the head, into Christ' (Eph. 4:15). Then Paul uses the image of the human body to describe the functioning and upbuilding of the church, the body of Christ: 'the whole body, joined and knit together by every joint with which it is supplied, when each part is working properly, makes bodily growth and upbuilds itself in love' (Eph. 4:16).

The ingathering of all to be the kingdom of God involves a progressive submission to the authority of Jesus. It is a submission of love, shaped and informed by the Spirit of God. God's plan 'for the fullness of time ... is to unite all things in him [Christ], things in heaven and things on earth' (Eph. 1:10). This is the mystery hidden from all ages. The Church is called to be a sign of this kingdom in formation. So the Catholic Catechism says: 'The Church in this world is the sacrament of salvation, the sign and the instrument of the communion of God and of men'.[9]

The full ingathering of the redeemed will only be realized with the coming of the Lord. Jesus gives the image that 'many will come from east and west and sit at table with Abraham, Isaac and Jacob in the kingdom of heaven' (Matt. 8:11). This ingathering will not be complete until the Jewish people have come to recognize their Messiah. 'The glorious Messiah's coming is suspended at every moment of history until his recognition by "all Israel"'.[10] Only then will occur the resurrection of the body, which will complete the work of our salvation and the full ingathering of the servants of God.[11]

THE NEW ADAM

*In whom are hid all the treasures of
wisdom and knowledge (Col. 2:3)*

As the Holy Spirit leads the Church of Jesus
Christ deeper into the Father's heart, opening up
the eternal perspective of his purposes from before
creation, deeper aspects to the person of Jesus
begin to emerge. This deepening in relation to
Jesus has two distinct dimensions: one, a deeper
understanding of his passion and death; the other,
a deeper understanding of Jesus as himself the new
Adam, the new creation, in whom 'the whole
fullness of deity dwells bodily' (Col. 2:9).

We have seen that Paul only comes to use the term
'mystery' after some years of apostolic ministry.
Mystery represents his deepening understanding of
the eternal plan of the Father. While Paul's
understanding is still totally Christo-centric, the

teaching in the later epistles, especially Ephesians and Colossians, expands to take in the full panorama of God's plan of creation and redemption. The cross-resurrection is still at the centre of the message, but it is now seen to stand at the centre of all history too, human and cosmic.

A Deeper Understanding of the Cross

As Paul is led into a deeper understanding of God's purposes, so he comes to a deeper understanding of the cross of Christ. It is not that he always fully understands the message of the cross and redemption, which is later presented in a larger framework. Prayerful reflection on the whole biblical revelation enables Paul to penetrate more deeply the extraordinary self-emptying of Jesus in the incarnation and particularly in his passion and death.

From the beginning of his ministry, Paul sought to prove that 'Jesus was the Christ' (Acts 9:22), preaching that 'the Christ must suffer' (Acts 26:23). We find an account of Paul's earlier preaching of the good news in Acts 13:16-41. The account of the death of Jesus is somewhat oblique: 'Though they could charge him with nothing deserving death, yet they asked Pilate to have him killed. And when they had fulfilled all that was written of him, they took him down from the tree, and laid him in a tomb' (Acts 13:28-29). The heart of the message is the resurrection - 'but God raised him from the dead' (Acts 13:30).

Paul's deeper understanding of the death of Jesus is manifested when he begins to preach about 'the cross'. This first appears in the letters to the Corinthians and the letter to the Galatians. Paul now directly associates the gospel with the cross: 'For Christ did not send me to baptize but to preach the gospel, and not with eloquent wisdom, lest the cross of Christ be emptied of its power' (1 Cor. 1:17). In Galatians, Paul presents the Christian life as a union with Jesus in his crucifixion: 'I have been crucified with Christ; for it is no longer I who live, but Christ who lives in me; and the life I now live in the flesh I live by faith in the Son of God, who loved me and gave himself for me' (Gal. 2:20). So he ends this letter by writing: 'But far be it from me to glory except in the cross of our Lord Jesus Christ, by which the world has been crucified to me, and I to the world' (Gal. 6:14).

It is in 2 Corinthians and in Galatians that Paul enters new territory in the shocking way that he speaks of the identification of Jesus with sinners on the cross. He says in Galatians: 'Christ redeemed us from the curse of the law, having become a curse for us' (Gal. 3:13). Equally astonishing is the statement in 2 Corinthians: 'We beseech you on behalf of Christ, be reconciled to God. For our sake he made him to be sin who knew no sin, so that in him we might become the righteousness of God' (2 Cor. 5:20-21). If these expressions were not found in the New Testament - become a curse, made sin - we would probably reject them as extreme. They confront us with what in Philippians is called the *kenosis*, the self-emptying of Jesus: '[he] emptied himself, taking the form of a slave [*doulos*], being born in the likeness of men. And being found in human form he humbled himself and became obedient unto death, even death on a cross' (Phil. 2:7-8).

Here all rational explanations fall woefully short. The great Catholic theologian Hans Urs von Balthasar warns against two extremes: 'that of interpreting the suffering of Christ as a punitive raging of divine anger against the innocent victim

... and that of seeing this suffering as merely the manifestation of the superabundance of divine love'.[1] The first is too extrinsic, too legal, too much of a quid pro quo, a tit-for-tat view of God's dealing with sin. The second is too sentimental, not facing the degree of abandonment and desolation in the human experience of Jesus.

There is a divine wrath, and there is infinite divine love, manifested in the cross. But it is not the wrath of the Father and the love of the Son. It is the wrath of God - Father, Son and Holy Spirit - and the even greater love of God - Father, Son and Holy Spirit. It is God's total engagement with humanity and the world; it is entering through love into the depths of human misery, into the abyss of human alienation, into the horror of meaning-lessness. Jesus 'tastes' death for everyone (see Heb. 2:9). He lives the absolute consequence of sin: the dereliction, the absence, the nothingness. He clings on in his spirit through blind faith and trust. 'But thou, O Lord, be not far off! O thou my help, hasten to my aid' (Ps. 22:19).

It is now that we can glimpse the significance of the descent of Jesus to the abode of the dead. This was thought important enough to include in the first

official creed of the Church: 'He descended into
hell.' It is a consequence of the total identification
of Jesus with suffering humanity that he
experiences what all humans before him have
experienced in their death. This is not so much a
triumphant descent in the spirit, as the completion
of the kenosis. He drinks the cup to the end. The
triumph only comes with the intervention of God to
vindicate his totally obedient Son, torn apart in his
humanity by the sundering of death.

The Newness of the Glorified Jesus

The perspective of 'mystery', of God's plan from
before the beginning, leads to a deeper
understanding of the Son of God in his eternal
reality and in his humanity transformed in the
resurrection. This is expressed, for example, in the
extolling of Christ in the first chapter of Colossians:
'He is the image of the invisible God, the first-born
of all creation' (Col. 1:15). This is a statement
about the divinity of Christ, for the next verse
mentions his role in creation. But then, three
verses later, we move on to the incarnation. 'He is
the head of the body, the church; he is the
beginning, the first-born from the dead, that in
everything he might be pre-eminent' (Col. 1:18).

The first-born in eternity becomes the first-born
from the dead. In the resurrection, a new world is
born. In the resurrection, there is a new creation.
'But in fact Christ has been raised from the dead,
the first fruits of those who have fallen asleep' (1
Cor. 15:20). It is in this context that Paul compares
Jesus to Adam: 'For as in Adam all die, so also in
Christ shall all be made alive' (1 Cor. 15:22). Later
on in this chapter, Paul takes up the Adam
comparison again: 'Thus it is written, "The first
man Adam became a living being"; the last Adam
became a life-giving spirit' (1 Cor. 15:45).

Here there is both a comparison and a
transcending. As Adam was the head of the first
humanity, so Jesus Christ is the head of the new
humanity. But whereas Adam was only a
beginning, Jesus is both the new beginning and the
completion. Jesus is 'the first and the last', the
Alpha and the Omega (Rev. 1:17; 2:8). In his
humanity is embodied the Father's full purpose for
us all. 'For in him all the fullness of God was
pleased to dwell' (Col. 1:19); 'For in him the whole
fullness of deity dwells bodily' (Col. 2:9).

In his death, Jesus was made a curse for us, he was
made sin for us. But in his resurrection, God has

made Jesus 'our wisdom, our righteousness and sanctification and redemption' (1 Cor. 1:30). The perfection of humanity is now realized in Jesus. Everything beautiful, everything admirable and desirable, everything clever and wise, everything creative and inspiring is in him. Everything we have yet to learn and discover for our lives, we are to learn and receive from him. Paul prays for the Christians in Colossae and in Laodicea 'that their hearts may be encouraged as they are knit together in love, to have all the riches of assured understanding and the knowledge of God's mystery, of Christ, in whom are hid all the treasures of wisdom and knowledge' (Col. 2:2-3).

This perspective of God's mystery demands a great humility in every Christian. Yes, we have been given the most wonderful heritage, the Word of God, the gift of the Holy Spirit, the body and the blood of the Lord. Yet we know so little. We understand so inadequately the great gifts we have been given. But we are in Christ, who knows all. We are invited to enter more deeply, to penetrate further into him who is the fulfilment of all things.

The Gospel of John

In this book, I am not making so many references
to the Gospel of John, primarily because John does
not use the language of mystery. On the other
hand, John's Gospel, being much later than the
others, and the fruit of long years of contemplation
on the Jesus-event, presents us with the life of
Jesus from the eternal perspective. Jesus is the
Word, who 'was with God and who was God' (John
1:1), 'who was in the beginning with God' (John 1:
2). This is precisely the perspective of mystery in
Paul.

In John's Gospel we find an extraordinary
combination. We find the divinity of Jesus much
more clearly expressed, and we find the human
qualities and characteristics of Jesus more sharply
delineated. Much more is revealed about the
relationship of Jesus to his heavenly Father. He is
the Son who only does 'what he sees the Father
doing' (John 5:19), the one on whom 'the Father
[has] set his seal' (John 6:27), who knows him 'for I
come from him' (John 7:29), who speaks of what he
has 'seen with the Father' (John 8:38), who dares to
say, 'I and the Father are one' (John 10:30). It is

only from John that we hear about the marriage feast at Cana, to which it seems Jesus was invited because of his mother (John 2:1-2), that we are told that 'Jesus did not trust himself' to many who believed in him (John 2:24), that we have the shortest verse in the Bible 'Jesus wept' (John 11:35), that we know that Jesus often met with his disciples in the Garden of Gethsemane (John 18:2). Similarly, we learn from John that Judas kept the money box (John 13:29).

The eternal perspective with its focus on the divinity of Jesus does not diminish his humanity, but rather it gives added significance to each human detail. To enter more deeply into the mystery is never to become esoteric and distance oneself from everyday reality.

Deeper into the Trinity

In this revelation of the mystery, hidden from all ages, the one God who is Father, Son and Holy Spirit is being revealed. The secret now unveiled is that God has a Son, a beloved Son. This Son becomes man, being 'conceived by the power of the Holy Spirit, and born of the Virgin Mary'.[2] The letter to the Ephesians is strongly trinitarian. The

Son comes to us from the Father in and through the Spirit: 'that ... he (the Father) may grant you to be strengthened with might through his Spirit ... to know the love of Christ' (Eph. 3:16-17). The Spirit then leads us back to the Father in and through the Spirit: 'for through him [Christ] we both have access in one Spirit to the Father' (Eph. 2:18). The strongly trinitarian teaching also emphasizes unity: 'There is one body and one Spirit ... one Lord, one faith, one baptism, one God and Father of us all, who is above all and through all and in all.' (Eph. 4:4-6). Therefore as Christians we live in 'the grace of the Lord Jesus Christ, the love of God and the fellowship of the Holy Spirit' (2 Cor. 13:14).

We should understand the opening up of the mystery as itself the work of the Holy Spirit.[3] It is a fulfilment of the trinitarian promise in John's Gospel: 'But the Counsellor, the Holy Spirit, whom the Father will send in my name, he will teach you all things, and bring to your remembrance all that I have said to you' (John 14:26).

The Mystery of the Gospel

It is significant that being led deeper into the mystery of Christ involves both a deeper

understanding of the cross and the self-emptying of
Jesus, and a deeper entry into who Jesus is and his
relationship with the Father. Christian faith is in
no way a form of gnosis, or salvation by knowledge,
in which believers leave behind the elementary
steps and graduate to something higher. No,
Christians always need to hear again the basic
gospel. We always need to hear the whole Word of
God. In this life, we always remain sinners in need
of repentance and forgiveness. Yet, even in our
weakness - indeed as we discover our weakness -
we are led into the depths of the Father's plan. As
Paul said, 'I will all the more gladly boast of my
weaknesses, that the power of Christ may rest upon
me' (2 Cor. 12:9).

It is in this context that we can see the significance
of Paul's phrase in Ephesians 'the mystery of the
gospel' (Eph. 6:9). This phrase occurs in a passage
in many ways characteristic of Ephesians where
Paul teaches about the spiritual battle against 'the
spiritual hosts of wickedness in the heavenly places'
(6:12) and the need for the Christians to 'put on the
whole armour of God' (6:11) and to 'pray at all
times in the Spirit' (6:18). The Ephesians are then
urged to make supplication also for him, 'that

utterance may be given me in opening my mouth boldly to proclaim the mystery of the gospel, for which I am an ambassador in chains' (6:19-20). The mystery is not something beyond the gospel. As Paul has been led into the eternal plan of God, he sees more clearly the depths of the gospel. We might say: we are led from the gospel into the mystery, and then back deeper into the mystery of the gospel.

Part III

The Mystery of the Church

THE MYSTERY OF ISRAEL

*For God has consigned all men to
disobedience, that he might have mercy
upon all (Rom. 11:32)*

As we probe more thoroughly the mystery of
Christ, we need to look more closely at the place of
the Jewish people. For in Rom. 11:25, Paul uses
the word 'mystery' of Israel. It comes near the end
of the three chapters (Rom. 9-11), in which Paul
reflects on the tragic situation of his own people.
The Israelites were chosen by God to be his own
people. They had been given many gifts, many
promises: 'They are Israelites, and to them belong
the sonship, the glory, the covenants, the giving of
the law, the worship, and the promises; to them
belong the patriarchs, and of their race, according
to the flesh, is the Christ' (Rom. 9:4-5).

The Problem

In these chapters, Paul is wrestling with an immense question. Paul is himself a Jew, chosen to be the apostle to the Gentiles.[1] Like every zealous Jew, Paul believed that God will one day send a redeemer, the Messiah, the son of David, who will deliver Israel from its oppressors and reign in Jerusalem on the throne of his father David. The Messiah-King will inaugurate a reign of righteousness. This expectation is at the heart of Jewish faith: it shines out from the prophetic songs of Mary and of Zechariah in the first chapter of Luke's Gospel.

The disciples of Jesus, all Jews, had come to confess him as the Messiah of Israel. Peter says at Caesarea Philippi, 'You are the Christ, the son of the living God' (Matt. 16:16). The hope of the Jewish disciples is severely dented by the crucifixion of Jesus: on the road to Emmaus two of them confess that 'we had hoped that he was the one to redeem Israel' (Luke 24:21). Their hope is rekindled as they recognize the risen Jesus, but then they wonder - very naturally for Jews - when he is going to fulfil the Messianic mission of restoring the kingdom to Israel (Acts 1:6).

On the major Jewish feast of Shavuot (Pentecost), a great crowd of Jews, both born Jews and the converts known as proselytes, gather in Jerusalem for the celebration of the feast. The Holy Spirit is poured out upon the disciples, and Simon Peter declares to the crowd: 'Let all the house of Israel therefore know assuredly that God has made him both Lord and Christ [Messiah], this Jesus whom you crucified' (Acts 2:36). This news creates a stir. About three thousand Jews accept the gospel that day (Acts 2:41). The good news continues to spread among the chosen people. 'And the word of God increased; and the number of the disciples multiplied greatly in Jerusalem, and a great many of the priests were obedient to the faith' (Acts 6:7).

We first meet Paul under his original name of Saul of Tarsus. Saul was a fierce persecutor 'ravaging the church' (Acts 8:3) and 'breathing threats and murder against the disciples of the Lord' (Acts 9:1). On his way to Damascus to arrest any disciples he should find, he has a blinding revelation of Jesus. He ends up doing the opposite of what he went to Damascus to do. Saul 'confounded the Jews who lived in Damascus by proving that Jesus was the Christ' (Acts 9:22).

However, despite this growth in the Church, only a relatively small percentage of the Jews come to faith in Jesus as the Messiah of Israel. What percentage we do not know. But the followers of Jesus find themselves a minority. This presents the Jewish disciples with a big dilemma. How is it possible that the Jewish people, chosen as God's own, destined to bring the Messiah into the world, should not all have recognized Jesus as Messiah when he came? This eventuality is unimaginable for the Jews - that their Messiah should come and they would not recognize him. There is in fact a double Jewish failure to accept Jesus: first, in his public ministry, though crowds follow him for a time; second, the refusal of the majority to accept the testimony of the disciples after his resurrection. The situation is further complicated when the crucified and risen Saviour, rejected by the majority of the Jews, is accepted by increasing numbers of pagans.

This is the dilemma troubling Paul, as it was surely disturbing other Jewish believers in Jesus. What is different about Paul is that he leaves a written description of the agony over his fellow Jews that is tearing at his heart. He gives us this account in the letter to the Romans.

The Letter to the Romans

Christians have often read the epistle to the
Romans as though chapters 9 to 11 about the
Jewish people form a diversion from the main
theme of the letter. In this reading, the first eight
chapters provide Paul's basic teaching on
justification by faith and Chapters 12 to 16 provide
the practical application of that teaching. Chapters
9 to 11 then appear as an interruption or a
diversion from the overall theme. Scholars today
increasingly recognize that this is a wrong way to
read Romans. The relationship between Jews and
Gentiles is central to the whole letter.

The overall theme is indicated in Rom. 1: 'For I am
not ashamed of the gospel: it is the power of God for
salvation to every one who has faith, to the Jew
first and also to the Greek' (vv.16). Paul introduces
here the central theme of justification through faith
(see also v.17), as well as the relationship between
Jew and Gentile. Both are equally in need of God's
mercy: 'For there is no distinction: since all have
sinned and fall short of the glory of God, they are
justified by his grace as a gift, through the
redemption which is in Christ Jesus' (Rom. 3:22-

24). The Jews have an advantage: they 'are
entrusted with the oracles of God' (Rom. 3:2). But
they do not have a privileged way to salvation. The
teaching on baptism and on sharing in Christ's
death so as to share in his resurrection applies to
Jew and Gentile alike. But a big question remains:
how is it that the Jews 'entrusted with the oracles
of God' have failed to receive this salvation which
they themselves had announced?

Paul's Three Questions

This question is an agonizing one for Paul. Paul is
in anguish because his own people have not
recognized their own Messiah: 'my conscience bears
me witness in the Holy Spirit, that I have great
sorrow and unceasing anguish in my heart' (Rom.
9:1-2). He is proud of being an Israelite: 'I myself
am an Israelite, a descendant of Abraham, a
member of the tribe of Benjamin' (Rom. 11:1). He
calls the Jews 'my brethren, my kinsmen by race'
(Rom. 9:3).

Paul is not just suffering over a great disappoint-
ment. He is wrestling with many questions: How
could such a thing happen? What does it mean?
What is going to happen to the Jewish people? In

chapters 9 to 11 of the letter to the Romans, we are privileged to be allowed inside Paul's heart as he grapples with these questions before the Lord. In these three chapters he poses three questions, to all of which he gives an answer of faith: 'By no means!' Absolutely not!

The first question is: 'Is there injustice on God's part?' (Rom. 9:14). This is a very Jewish question, a question asked by one of the chosen. It is the same as the implied question behind verse 6: 'But it is not as though the word of God had failed' (Rom. 9:6). It could easily seem to the Jew who believes in Jesus as the Messiah that the general Jewish failure to believe in Jesus represents a failure in the promise, that God has not kept his word to Israel. To all these thoughts, Paul says a clear 'No'. In denying any injustice on God's part, Paul introduces the idea of God's mercy. He quotes Ex. 33:19, saying, 'it depends not upon man's will or exertion, but upon God's mercy' (Rom. 9:16).

The second question is: 'Has God rejected his people?' (Rom. 11:1). Paul's answer again is 'By no means!' Certainly not. This answer is the opposite of what Christians have said through most of the centuries since Christ. Most Christians, including several Fathers of the Church, said that God had rejected the Jews, because they had rejected Jesus as the Messiah. In this view, sometimes called the replacement or the substitution teaching, the Church has taken the place of Israel as God's chosen covenant people. But Paul's answer is clear. 'God has not rejected his people whom he foreknew' (Rom. 11:2). His main argument is provided by the Jewish believers in Jesus. Though they are a minority among the Jewish people, their existence disproves the view that God has rejected the Jews. Just as in the days of Elijah, there were seven thousand who did not succumb to Baal worship, 'so too at the present time there is a remnant, chosen by grace' (Rom. 11:5). Paul is referring to the Jewish believers in Jesus. There is a tragedy here. 'Israel failed to obtain what it sought. The elect obtained it, but the rest were hardened' (Rom. 11:7).

The third question is the obvious sequel: What about the rest of the Jews who were hardened? Paul puts it this way: 'Have they stumbled so as to fall?' (Rom. 11:11).[2] In other words, have they so totally fallen away that they cannot be raised up and restored? Have they no more future in God?

Again Paul's answer is clear: 'By no means!' At this point Paul argues that God has used the unbelief of the Jews to bless the Gentiles: 'through their [the Jews'] trespass salvation has come to the Gentiles' (Rom. 11:11). This leads to a prophetic declaration about the future: 'if their trespass means riches for the world, and if their failure means riches for the Gentiles, how much more will their full inclusion mean!' (Rom. 11:12). In fact, the phrase 'full inclusion' is one word in Greek: *plērōma*, meaning fullness. Paul is predicting a future fullness for Israel, and saying this will be an even greater blessing to the nations than Israel's unbelief.

Paul makes a similar prediction in verse 15. 'For if their rejection means the reconciliation of the world, what will their acceptance mean but life from the dead?' (Rom. 11:15). There is a translation problem here, as Paul has already made clear that God has not rejected the Jews. A better translation would be 'their setting aside'.[3] Despite the setting aside of the Jewish people as a whole, there will be a future 'acceptance' (*próslēmpsis*) that is in some way a resurrection from the dead.

The Olive Tree

Paul illustrates his teaching with the image of a natural olive tree. This tree is Israel. Judah and Jerusalem are addressed as an olive tree: 'The Lord once called you, "A green olive tree, fair with goodly fruit"' (Jer. 11:16). The image of an olive tree also appears in Zechariah 4:11-14, where the two branches of the olive are the two 'anointed' who 'stand by the Lord of the whole earth.'[4] It is from the olive that oil is made, oil that symbolizes the Holy Spirit and points to the Messiah, the anointed one. In Paul's image, some branches have been broken off from the natural olive, that is, the Jews who did not accept Jesus. The Gentiles are like 'wild olive shoots' from an uncultivated tree that are grafted into the natural olive.

Paul draws lessons from this comparison. First, the Gentiles must avoid all arrogance. 'You will say, "Branches were broken off so that I might be grafted in." That is true. They were broken off because of their unbelief, but you stand fast only through faith. So do not become proud, but stand in awe' (Rom. 11:19-20). Second, God can graft back in the severed branches; indeed, it is easier to reincorporate the natural branches 'into their own olive tree' than to graft in those from the wild olive (Rom. 11:23-24).

From Problem to Mystery

In grappling with these questions, Paul is led through prophetic enlightenment from the anguish of a huge problem to wonder before an amazing mystery. In Rom. 11:25 Paul describes this puzzle about the Jews and the Gentiles as 'this mystery'. This does not mean that it cannot be understood, but that it can only be understood through the light of divine revelation. 'I want you to understand this mystery, brethren.' And then he gives God's answer to the problem: 'a hardening has come upon part of Israel, until the full number of the Gentiles come in, and so all Israel will be saved' (Rom. 11:25-26). As 'mystery' this history is not just a tragedy, it is the unfolding of the plan of God. It is the way in which God has chosen to bring his salvation to all peoples.

The elements in the answer are then: (1) a hardening (*pōrōsis*) - another form of this word had already been used in 11:7; (2) a part of Israel - the hardening affects a part but not the whole of Israel;

(3) until - the hardening is only for a time; (4) the fullness (*plērōma*) of the Gentiles has come in; (5) all Israel will be saved. Being prophetic revelation, we do not and cannot fully understand what this means: particularly what the fullness of the Gentiles and what 'all Israel' mean. The *Catechism of the Catholic Church* links this passage with Ephesians 4:13, teaching that: 'The "full inclusion" of the Jews in the Messiah's salvation in the wake of "the full number of the Gentiles", will enable the People of God to achieve "the measure of the stature of the fulness of Christ", in which "God may be all in all"'.[5]

Paul refuses a logical 'either-or' answer as he ponders the mystery. The (unbelieving) Jews 'are enemies of God .. as regards the gospel', but 'as regards election they are beloved for the sake of their forefathers' (Rom. 11: 28). From one angle, they are resisting the gospel of Jesus. From another angle, they are still the chosen people, beloved by God because of their forefathers in faith. In our human minds, we find this difficult to hold together: enemies and beloved at one and the same time! But since human refusal is not on the same level as the gift of God, we are not called to a balancing act. What is unchangeable is the call: 'For the gifts and the call of God are irrevocable' (Rom. 11:29).

At the end of his reflection, Paul receives a deeper understanding of God's mercy. He sees the sinfulness and the disobedience of all, but he sees them now in the light of God's mercy: 'Just as you [the Gentile believers] were once disobedient to God but now have received mercy because of their [the unbelieving Jews'] disobedience, so they have now been disobedient in order that by the mercy shown to you they may also receive mercy' (Rom. 11:30-31). There is no room for Gentile pride in relation to the Jews. The Gentiles are to behave in a way that makes the Jews jealous. Sadly, however, the long history of Christian treatment of the Jewish people has shown little mercy and has provided few grounds for them to become jealous.

From Anguish to Praise

Paul now comes full circle, we may say, from his starting point of great anguish over the unbelief of his kinsfolk. He is led deeper into the extraordinary mercy of God. He sees the disobedience of his people in a new light: 'For God has consigned all men to disobedience, that he may have mercy upon all' (Rom. 11:32). This launches the apostle on a great paean of praise, lauding the amazing greatness of our God: 'O the depth of the riches and wisdom and knowledge of God! How unsearchable are his judgments and how inscrutable his ways! For who has known the mind of the Lord or who has been his counsellor?' (Rom. 11: 33-34).

This is an important model for all Christian puzzlement over the ways of the Lord. When we think that the unthinkable has happened, that the bottom has fallen out of our world, we are to do what Paul did: turn to the Lord, even in anguished prayer. And we will be led to see the hand of the Lord even in the greatest human tragedy.

The Jews of Later Generations

What I have presented in this chapter is Paul's teaching about the Jewish people, and the refusal of the majority to accept Jesus as the Messiah. This teaching is not to be applied in every detail to the Jews of later generations in their continued refusal to believe in Jesus. For the refusal of later generations of Jews to accept the claims of Jesus owes much to the unchristlike behaviour of Christians towards the Jewish people. The obstacle to Jewish faith in Jesus presented by Christian behaviour towards the Jews has been stated very strongly by Cardinal Jean-Marie Lustiger, the Archbishop of Paris, himself a Jewish disciple of Jesus, in a recently published book: 'The Gentile [pagan] Christians killed the Jews under the pretext that they had killed the Christ; this is a manifest blasphemy, a clear revelation that it was the spirit of the world and not the Spirit of Christ that animated them. They acted under the power of Satan, who "is a murderer from the beginning" (John 8: 44). Thus they are responsible for the fact that the Messiah is unrecognizable and misunderstood by the Jews as by the pagans.'[6]

ONE NEW MAN

The Gentiles are fellow heirs (Eph. 3:6)

In Eph. 3, Paul speaks again of 'the mystery of Christ' (Eph. 3:4). Whereas he had spoken in Rom.11 of the mystery that is Israel, he speaks more specifically in Ephesians of the inclusion of the Gentiles in the mystery of Messiah. The eternal plan of the Father is that the Gentiles, the peoples of the nations throughout the world, will be brought in to share the blessings of the chosen people. So, the mystery is 'how the Gentiles are fellow heirs, members of the same body, and partakers of the promise in Christ Jesus through the gospel' (Eph. 3:6).

Old Testament Prophecies

The blessing of the Gentiles through Israel is

foreshadowed from the beginning of the history of the chosen people. In the original call to Abraham, God promised that 'by you all the families of the earth shall bless themselves' (Gen. 12:3). Following the severe testing of Abraham as to his willingness to sacrifice Isaac, the son of the promise, the Lord said, 'by your descendants shall all the nations of the earth bless themselves, because you have obeyed my voice' (Gen. 22:18). The same promise is made to Isaac in Gen. 26:4.

The blessing of the nations is an essential element in God's choice of a people to be his own in a unique way. Israel is called to be holy for the sake of the eventual holiness of all peoples. This is particularly expressed in the idea of Israel as a priestly people. In this passage from Exodus the whole earth and all its peoples are mentioned in the context of Israel's calling: 'Now therefore, if you will obey my voice and keep my covenant, you shall be my own possession among all peoples; for all the earth is mine, and you shall be to me a kingdom of priests and a holy nation' (Ex. 19:5-6).

The universal scope of Israel's calling is extolled in Israel's worship. Psalm 67 expresses this very clearly, beginning and ending with 'us', the people of Israel, leading the nations to praise the Lord:

> May God be gracious to us and bless us
>> and make his face to shine upon us,
> That thy way may be known upon earth,
>> thy saving power among all nations.
> Let the peoples praise thee, O God;
>> let all the peoples praise thee!
> Let the nations be glad and sing for joy,
>> for thou dost judge the peoples with equity
>> and guide the nations upon earth.
> Let the peoples praise thee, O God;
>> let all the peoples praise thee!
> The earth has yielded its increase;
>> God, our God, has blessed us.
> God has blessed us;
>> let all the ends of the earth fear him!

In the book of Isaiah the coming age of Messianic fulfilment includes blessing for the Gentiles. The blessing to the nations comes through their relationship to the chosen people, and particularly to the holy city of Jerusalem. 'It shall come to pass in the latter days that the mountain of the house of the Lord shall be established as the highest of the mountains, and shall be raised above the hills; and all the nations shall flow to it, and many peoples shall come, and say: "Come, let us go up to the mountain of the Lord, to the house of the God of Jacob; that he may teach us his ways and that we may walk in his paths"' (Is. 2:2-3).

In the second servant song in the second part of Isaiah, the Lord says to the servant: 'It is too light a thing that you should be my servant to raise up the tribes of Jacob and to restore the preserved of Israel; I will give you as a light to the nations, that my salvation may reach to the end of the earth' (Is. 49:6). This passage indicates the servant role of Israel (the servant is addressed as Israel in verse 3), whereas the third section of Isaiah from chapter 56[1] mostly presents the nations as the servants of Israel. Here the nations will be brought to Jerusalem: 'my house shall be called a house of prayer for all peoples' (Is. 56:7). 'For behold, darkness shall cover the earth, and thick darkness the peoples; but the Lord will arise upon you [Jerusalem], and his glory will be seen upon you. And nations shall come to your light, and kings to the brightness of your rising' (Is. 60:2-3).

It is true that the nations are also presented in the Old Testament as the enemies of Israel. The first commands to Israel concerning whole nations were strongly negative. Israel's formation as God's people required a setting apart and a cleansing from the idolatry and immorality of the surrounding peoples. Against this background of hostility we can see how remarkable was Israel's positive vision for the nations. The negative view of the nations as the enemies of Israel of course continues, and corresponds to Israel's experience of invasion by pagan powers. God will enter into judgement with the nations (see, for example, Joel 3), but even here the prophet Zechariah says that 'every one that survives of all the nations that have come against Jerusalem shall go up year after year to worship the King, the Lord of hosts, and to keep the feast of booths' (Zech. 14:16).

The Mission of Jesus

The mission of Jesus fits harmoniously within the vision of Israel in the Old Testament. We often do not understand this, because as Gentile Christians we usually begin from the incarnation as an event of universal significance. We easily accept Jesus Christ as Son of God and Saviour of the world without perhaps thinking of his role within Israel. But during his earthly ministry Jesus understands his mission within the framework of his own people. When he sends out the twelve, Jesus tells them: 'Go nowhere among the Gentiles, and enter no town of the Samaritans, but go rather to the lost sheep of the house of Israel' (Matt. 10:5-6). When the Canaanite woman from the district of Tyre and Sidon seeks help for her daughter, the first reaction of Jesus is to see this request as incompatible with his mission: 'I was sent only to the lost sheep of the house of Israel' (Matt. 15:24). His reply to the woman's insistent demands seems to express the disdain of the Jews for the unclean Gentiles or *goyim*: 'It is not fair to take the children's bread and throw it to the dogs' (Matt. 15:26). Why is Jesus moved to accede to the woman's request by her response to this rebuff? Did her acceptance of the image of the dogs eating 'the crumbs that fall from their masters' table' include a recognition of the special calling of Israel?

It seems clear that Jesus understands his mission before his passion as a preaching of the kingdom to his own people. Yet he is clearly aware of an openness to the Gentiles in the Old Testament. He angers the people of Nazareth by speaking of the ministry of Elijah and Elisha to Gentiles: 'But in truth, I tell you, there were many widows in Israel in the days of Elijah, when the heaven was shut up three years and six months, when there came a great famine over all the land; and Elijah was sent to none of them but only to Zarephath, in the land of Sidon, to a woman who was a widow. And there were many lepers in Israel in the time of the prophet Elisha; and none of them was cleansed, but only Naaman the Syrian' (Luke 4:25-27). And, in contrast to his dealings with the Canaanite woman, Jesus heals the servant of a centurion, saying of the centurion that 'not even in Israel have I found such faith', adding 'I tell you, many will come from east and west and sit at table with Abraham, Isaac, and Jacob in the kingdom of heaven' (Matt. 8:10-11).

A quite different instruction to the apostles is found at the end of Matthew's Gospel. Here Jesus tells them, 'Go therefore and make disciples of all nations, baptizing them in the name of the Father and of the Son and of the Holy Spirit' (Matt. 28:19). It seems likely that this passage is a subsequent formulation, reflecting later liturgical usage with its explicitly trinitarian formula. But this post-resurrection instruction is not incompatible with the specific mission of Jesus to Israel, because theologically the universal mission of Jesus is rooted in his death and resurrection.

The relation between the mission of Jesus to Israel and his mission to all peoples can only be rightly understood when we realize that Jesus identified himself fully with the call and the mission of Israel. This identification is first expressed at his circumcision on the eighth day after his birth, when Jesus is physically marked with the sign of the covenant. It is affirmed at his baptism in the Jordan, when he who is without sin receives John's baptism of repentance. In fact, John says, 'for this I came baptizing with water, that he might be revealed to Israel' (John 1:31). It is realized above all in his passion and death, when Jesus enters totally into the suffering servant call of Israel, foretold so remarkably in Isaiah 52 and 53.[2] This is expressed in the prophecy of Caiaphas, that 'Jesus should die for the nation, and not for the nation only, but to gather into one the children of God who are scattered abroad' (John 11:51-52). In this way, Jesus embodies the call of Israel to be a blessing and a light to the nations. In and through Jesus, Israel will bless the Gentiles. The Servant-Messiah of Israel becomes the Saviour of the world.

Light for Revelation to the Gentiles

The old man Simeon had prophesied that the child of Mary would be a 'light for revelation to the Gentiles' (Luke 2:32). It is not many years after the birth of the Church at Pentecost that the first non-Jews come to faith and are baptized.[3] In the Acts of the Apostles, we can see a steady moving out from the Jewish kernel of the Church, a movement already indicated in the instruction to be 'my witnesses in Jerusalem and in all Judea and Samaria and to the end of the earth' (Acts 1:8). The Ethiopian eunuch baptized by Philip, who 'had come to Jerusalem to worship' (Acts 8:27), is no doubt a 'God-fearer' unable as a eunuch to become a proselyte.

The big breakthrough comes in Caesarea with the conversion of Cornelius and his household. It is striking how Luke emphasizes the guidance of the Holy Spirit from beginning to end of this process - through visions, heavenly voices and the Spirit's interruption of Peter's preaching. The Spirit prepares Cornelius to receive Peter and his message, and the Spirit prepares Peter through the vision of the lowered sheet containing animals, clean and unclean. After the 'Holy Spirit fell on all who heard the word' (Acts 10:44), we are told: 'And the believers from among the circumcised who came with Peter were amazed, because the gift of the Holy Spirit had been poured out even on the Gentiles' (Acts 10:45).

Why were the Jewish believers astonished? Remember that Cornelius was a 'God-fearer', a Gentile who had not converted to Judaism but who attended the synagogue. He is emphatically not a 'heathen', but 'a devout man who feared God with all his household, gave alms liberally to the people, and prayed constantly to God' (Acts 10:2). The surprise of the Jews is that the Holy Spirit is poured out on those outside the chosen people of the covenant. The promise of the Spirit in the prophets was to Israel (see Jer. 31:33; Ez. 36:26-28). Yet here the Gentiles receive the same gift as the Jews and in the same way, 'just as we have' (Acts 10:47).[4]

Very soon after, we are told of Jewish believers from Cyprus and Cyrene who preach the Lord Jesus to the Greeks in Antioch (see Acts 11:20). This bold evangelization is very effective. 'And the hand of the Lord was with them, and a great number that believed turned to the Lord' (Acts 11:21). The developments in Caesarea and in Antioch quickly become known in Jerusalem, giving rise to lively debate and controversy. There is opposition from those Luke calls 'the circumcision party' (Acts 11:2). Some even travel to Antioch to insist on conversion to Judaism, saying: 'Unless you are circumcised according to the custom of Moses, you cannot be saved' (Acts 15:1). The leadership in Jerusalem has the wisdom to send to Antioch Barnabas, who had already demonstrated his openness to unexpected moves of the Holy Spirit in welcoming the new convert, Saul of Tarsus (see Acts 9:27; 11:22). After recognizing the work of the Holy Spirit in the Gentile converts of Antioch, Barnabas brings Saul from Tarsus, no doubt aware that Saul, soon to be Paul, had been designated by the Lord as 'a chosen instrument of mine to carry my name before the Gentiles' (Acts 9:15). Barnabas and Paul teach in Antioch for a year, and, we are told, it was 'in Antioch the disciples were for the first time called Christians (Acts 11:26).[5]

The controversies in Antioch over the growing Gentile membership lead the church there to send to Jerusalem a group of leaders, including Paul and

Barnabas. 'The apostles and elders were gathered together to consider this matter' (Acts 15:6). Important contributions are made by Peter, who witnesses to the work of the Holy Spirit in Caesarea, and by Barnabas and Paul, who do the same for Antioch. The resolution to the controversy is proposed by James, the leader of the church in Jerusalem.[6] This proposal is remarkably generous, and is accepted by all. The Gentile believers are welcomed into the Church as full members, with as few ritual burdens being imposed as possible: 'it has seemed good to the Holy Spirit and to us to lay upon you no greater burden than these necessary things' (Acts 15:28).

Following the Jerusalem ruling, the evangelization and the conversion of the Gentiles proceed apace, especially through the ministry of Paul, the apostle to the Gentiles. This brings us to the situation in the church of Ephesus, where there were both Jewish and Gentile believers.

The Mystery of Messiah

How do we know that there were Jewish and Gentile members of the church in Ephesus? For Ephesus, this is not just well-founded conjecture.

For the letter to the Ephesians speaks sometimes of 'us' and sometimes of 'you'. The references in the early chapters to 'us' mean the Jewish believers. So, 'we who first hoped in Christ' (Eph. 1:12) are the Jews who have accepted Jesus as the Messiah. The next verse speaks of 'you', addressing the Gentile believers: 'In him, you also, who have heard the word of truth' (Eph. 1:13). In this light, the statement of the apostle in verse 15 is particularly important: 'because I have heard of your faith in the Lord Jesus and your love towards all the saints' (Eph. 1:15). The Christian faith of the Gentiles in Ephesus is marked by their love for 'all the saints', for the Jewish believers as well as the Gentiles.

In chapter 2, Paul addresses the different situation of the Gentile converts from the Jewish. Here again the 'you' refers to the Gentiles: 'you Gentiles in the flesh' (Eph. 2:11). The conversion of a Gentile is significantly different from the conversion of a Jew. The situation of the Gentiles before conversion is described in stark terms: 'remember that you were at that time separated from Christ, alienated from the commonwealth of Israel, and strangers to the covenants of promise, having no hope and without God in the world' (Eph. 2:12).

But now through the blood of Jesus, the Christ, shed on the cross, the Gentiles who were far off have been brought near. Jesus 'has made us both one' (Eph. 2:14), that is, Jew and Gentile. He 'has broken down the dividing wall of hostility' (Eph. 2:14), reconciling 'both to God in one body through the cross' (Eph. 2:16). As a result, through Jesus, 'we both [Jew and Gentile] have access in one Spirit to the Father' (Eph. 1:18).

Then Paul describes the transformed condition of the Gentile believers. 'So then you are no longer strangers and sojourners, but you are fellow citizens with the saints and members of the household of God, built upon the foundation of the [Jewish] apostles and prophets, Christ [Messiah] Jesus himself being the cornerstone' (Eph. 2:19-20). This sets the scene for a further description of 'the mystery of Christ' at the beginning of chapter 3. I have headed this section 'the Mystery of Messiah', because the Jewish term 'Messiah' helps us better to enter into the mind of Paul and his close disciples, who were being led to understand more deeply the person and the mission of the Messiah of Israel.

As already mentioned, the term 'mystery' for Paul expresses the eternal plan of God, hidden through

the ages, but now made manifest in the Christ-
Messiah. So after chapter 2, Paul says: 'When you
read this you can perceive my insight into the
mystery of Christ' (Eph. 3:4). This mystery he then
spells out: 'that is, how the Gentiles are fellow
heirs, members of the same body, and partakers of
the promise in Christ Jesus through the gospel'
(Eph. 3:6). The Greek original has the prefixes '*syn*'
or '*sym*', which would be 'co-' in English or '*mit*' in
German.[8] So the Gentiles are co-heirs with the
Jews, 'co-body' with the Messiah, co-sharers in the
promise in Messiah Jesus.

Paul is saying something essential about the nature
of the Church. The Church is made up of Jew and
Gentile, reconciled through the blood of the cross.
Through the Messiah, the heritage of Israel is
transformed from within and the Gentiles are
admitted to become 'fellow citizens'[9] with the
sanctified Israelites. The Church is the body of
those reconciled through the blood of the Messiah,
but the archetypal division dealt with by the cross
is that between Jews and Gentiles. The result is
that the Church is 'one new man in place of the
two' (Eph. 2:15).

There may be many aspects of this mystery that we cannot yet understand. That should not surprise us.[10] One concerns the relationship between Jewish and Gentile believers within the Church. This has been made more difficult by the long centuries of Church insistence on Jewish converts abandoning all outward expression of their Jewishness. The teaching of Ephesians cannot mean that Jewish believers in Jesus have to cease being Jews. Here there is a parallel between Jews and Gentiles on the one hand, and men and women on the other hand. In Galatians, Paul had written: 'There is neither Jew nor Greek, there is neither slave nor free, there is neither male nor female; for you are all one in Christ Jesus' (Gal. 3:28). This cannot mean that converts are no longer Jews or Gentiles, any more than that converts are no longer men or women. Paul's teaching is that they all have equal access to salvation, and are made one in Christ Jesus, whatever their legal status or gender. The miracle of the Church's unity is that this great diversity is shaped and formed into harmony by the work of the cross.

Now we can see more clearly how God is bringing about his 'plan for the fullness of time to unite all things in him [Christ]' (Eph. 1:10). It is realized through the mission of the Messiah of Israel, who through his sacrificial death overcomes the hostility between Jew and Gentile, 'abolishing in his flesh the law of commandments and ordinances' (Eph. 2:15), forming the Church as the union of Jew and Gentile in his body. This body is 'the fullness of him who fills all in all' (Eph. 1:23). There is no other way in which all things can be brought together under Jesus Christ, than through the shedding of his blood and the reconciliation of Jew and Gentile that is the immediate fruit of the cross.

STEWARDS OF THE MYSTERIES OF GOD

I received from the Lord what I also delivered to you (1 Cor. 11:23)

In 1 Cor. 4, Paul describes how he would like to be regarded by the Christians: 'This is how one should regard us, as servants of Christ and stewards of the mysteries of God' (1 Cor. 4:1). Paul is not just a custodian of the Word of God, responsible for the doctrine being taught in the Church. He is also steward of a way of life and worship in the early Church. At the heart of this worship is the celebration of the Lord's Supper, the Eucharist.

What Paul hands on to his disciples he outlines at the beginning of 1 Cor. 15: 'For I delivered to you as of first importance what I also received' (1 Cor. 15:3). This message concerns Jesus, his death, burial and resurrection from the dead. But in chapter 11, he speaks about handing on the way the Eucharist is celebrated. 'For I received from the Lord what I also delivered to you, that the Lord Jesus on the night when he was betrayed took bread...' (1 Cor. 11:23). Paul is conscious of transmitting something precious. He has to hand on faithfully what he has received. This precious heritage concerns the life of Jesus and the teaching that he gave; it also concerns the actions of Jesus and all that he told the disciples to do in his name. 'Do this in remembrance of me' is repeated twice, once for the bread, once more for the cup (1 Cor. 11:24, 25).

The use of the word 'mysteries' in 1 Cor. 4 reflects what we now call this liturgical-sacramental dimension. It no doubt included everything symbolic/practical that Jesus entrusted to his disciples. We are told of the first believers in Jesus that 'they devoted themselves to the apostles' teaching and fellowship, to the breaking of bread and the prayers' (Acts 2:42). Their instructions would have included baptism and praying for the sick, as well as the celebration of the Supper of the Lord. The *Catechism of the Catholic Church* speaks of this formation in the mysteries: 'Liturgical catechesis aims to initiate people into the mystery of Christ ... by proceeding from the visible to the invisible, from the sign to the signified, from the "sacraments" to the "mysteries".[1]

First the Physical, then the Spiritual

In 1 Cor.15, Paul writes about the resurrection of the body: 'If there is a physical body, there is also a spiritual body. Thus it is written, "The first man Adam became a living being"; the last Adam became a life-giving spirit. But it is not the spiritual which is first but the physical, and then the spiritual' (1 Cor. 15:44-46). The comparison between the first and the last Adam suggests that Paul is here teaching a vital principle. Jesus becomes 'life-giving spirit' in his bodily ascension to glory. In his resurrection-ascension the humanity of Jesus is transformed from being a 'living being', anointed by the Holy Spirit, to a 'life-giving spirit', able to transmit the Holy Spirit. The physical provides the raw material for transformation by the Holy Spirit into the spiritual.

A parallel transformation of the physical order by the spiritual can also be observed in the two covenants. The new covenant is made with 'the house of Israel and the house of Judah' (Jer. 31:31), but unlike the earlier covenant, the Lord puts his law within them and writes it upon their hearts (Jer. 31:33). The new covenant is not a replacement covenant, that is, made with a different people; it is a transformative covenant, further transforming through the Holy Spirit those with whom the first covenant was made.

The same principle holds in relation to the kingdom of God. There is first a physical kingdom, built on King David; as a consequence, there can later be a spiritual kingdom, built upon the son of David, the Messiah of Israel. Jesus is first son of David at the natural level, in order that he can become through the Spirit of God the transformed son of David, the Messianic king, who 'will reign over the house of Jacob for ever' (Luke 1: 33).[2] The spiritual kingdom is not just an inspiring idea with no tangible kingdom reality. It is truly kingdom, transformed and reshaped through the death and resurrection of Jesus.

In the same way, a transformation took place in the practice of baptism. The Israelites had been 'baptized into Moses in the cloud and in the sea' (1 Cor. 10:2). There is a further development in the

Spirit from the baptism of John, which was a baptism unto repentance, to the baptism of Jesus, which is a baptism of 'water and the Spirit' (John 3:5).

A Formative Process

The process by which God selects the physical and prepares it for transformation into the spiritual is part of the schooling of God's people by the Spirit. 'Now before faith came, we were confined under the law, kept under restraint until faith should be revealed' (Gal. 3:23). The promises were given to Abraham and his offspring: 'But when the time had fully come, God sent forth his Son, born of woman, born under the law, to redeem those who were under the law, so that we might receive adoption as sons' (Gal. 4:4-5).

The rites of the Old Testament were part of this schooling. They represent the physical order established by the Lord, that is to be transformed from within by the Holy Spirit. Paul sees Jesus as the passover lamb, slain for the spiritual deliverance of his people: 'For Christ, our paschal lamb, has been sacrificed. Let us, therefore, celebrate the festival, not with the old leaven, the leaven of malice and evil, but with the unleavened bread of sincerity and truth' (1 Cor. 5:7-8). In Jesus, God has transformed the celebration of Passover from the inside. 'On the eve of his Passion, while still free, Jesus transformed this Last Supper with the apostles into the memorial of his voluntary offering to the Father for the salvation of men.'[3]

It is not the Church that changes the Jewish celebration of Passover. It is Jesus, who embodies in himself the calling of Israel, who transforms the Passover through his self-offering and its acceptance by the Father. It is another example of 'first the physical, and then the spiritual'. It is not a replacement of the physical by what is not physical. It is a transformation of the physical, that changes the character of the physical from within. This transformation from Passover to Eucharist is an intensification of the process of preparation for the fully physical-spiritual reality of the coming kingdom. 'By celebrating the Last Supper with his apostles in the course of the Passover meal, Jesus gave the Jewish Passover its definitive meaning. Jesus' passing over to his Father by his death and Resurrection, the new

Passover, is anticipated in the Supper and celebrated in the Eucharist, which fulfils the Jewish Passover and anticipates the final Passover of the Church in the glory of the kingdom.'[4]

The Age of the Church

The stewardship of the mysteries of Christ belongs to the age of the Church, the period between Pentecost and *parousia*. 'The gift of the Spirit ushers in a new era in the "dispensation of the mystery" - the age of the Church, during which Christ manifests, makes present, and communicates his work of salvation through the liturgy of his Church, "until he comes".'[5]

The age of the Church is the age of signs. Signs are still needed, because the spiritual reality to which the signs point - the glorified, ascended Jesus Christ - is not yet fully visible to our human sight. But the signs are more than the Old Testament signs, for the Messiah has come and has poured out his Spirit on the people of the covenant. They are signs that make present the risen Jesus as life-giving Spirit.

The liturgical signs are signs of faith. They express

the faith of the church community in the Lord
Jesus and in his ministry. The faith is expressed in
the Word of God, and in the sacramental actions
that make the promise of the Word present.
Vatican Two restated the essential connection
between Word of God and sacramental action: 'the
sacraments are sacraments of faith, drawing their
origin and nourishment from the Word.'[6]

The signs are to be repeated until the Lord comes.
So, of the Eucharist, Paul teaches: 'For as often as
you eat this bread and drink the cup, you proclaim
the Lord's death until he comes' (1 Cor. 11:26).
When the Lord comes in his glory, there will be no
further need for signs, because what the signs
signify will be fully made visible. Thus the
Eucharist is preparing the Church for the coming of
the Lord and his kingdom. As Pope John Paul says
in his latest encyclical letter: 'The Eucharist is a
straining towards the goal, a foretaste of the
fullness of joy promised by Christ (cf. John 15:11);
it is in some way the anticipation of heaven, the
"pledge of future glory". ... With the Eucharist we
digest, as it were, the "secret" of the resurrection.'[7]

The Faithful and Wise Steward

In the Gospel, the Lord asks the question: 'Who then is the faithful and wise steward, whom his master will set over his household, to give them their portion of food at the proper time?' (Luke 12:42). The responsibility of the steward is to feed the master's household. So, when Paul speaks of himself as a steward of the mysteries of God, he is referring to his responsibility as a minister of the Lord to feed the Lord's own people.

The language of mysteries indicates that the steward has the responsibility to feed the people with the food that the Lord himself gives. In the Old Testament, the Lord reproaches the shepherds for feeding themselves and not the sheep (Ezek. 34:8). In the Eucharist, the food provided is the body of the Lord 'given for you', the blood of the Lord 'shed for you and for all'. Just as the Word of God provides the meaning to the action of the shared communion, so the broken body and the shed blood of the Lord shape the ministry of the Word.

The minister commissioned to preach the Word of God is not being authorized to proclaim his own theological opinions to the world. Our personal views are thin fare for people who are hungering for the Word of the Lord. But limiting our preaching to the Word of God is not a boring restriction, leading only to the mouthing of biblical platitudes. It is first the discipline of feeding ourselves on the Word of the Lord, and not allowing ourselves to be more shaped by the world than by the Lord of all creation. As we feed on the Word of the Lord, we will want to submit our lives in faith to the incarnate Word, so that what comes out of our mouths is in very truth also the Word of the Lord. We first digest the Word, in order to live the Word. Only as we become Word from the one Word of God can we speak the Word with the power and the qualities of the Word.

Paul understood the preciousness of the Word and the urgency of preaching. 'I charge you,' he wrote to Timothy, 'in the presence of God and of Christ Jesus who is to judge the living and the dead, and by his appearing and his kingdom: preach the word, be urgent in season and out of season, convince, rebuke, and exhort, be unfailing in patience and in teaching' (2 Tim. 4:1-2).

Those of us called to be ministers of the Lord are entrusted with a treasure that is beyond our full understanding. We have to reverence the mystery that is bigger than ourselves, that envelops us and draws us into itself. In faith, we receive the mind and heart of the risen Saviour. Paul, the servant of Christ, knew what he had been given by the grace of the Lord: 'But we have the mind of Christ' (1 Cor. 2:16). In faith, we enter into the celebrations of the Church that already carry invisibly the reality of the coming kingdom. Each time, we celebrate the Eucharist, we hasten the day of the Lord's coming, when faith will give way to vision and signs to the glorious reality they signify. 'The Holy Spirit's transforming power in the liturgy hastens the coming of the kingdom and the consummation of the mystery of salvation. While we wait in hope he causes us really to anticipate the fullness of communion with the Holy Trinity'. [8]

As steward of the mysteries of Christ, the minister of the new covenant is responsible for the coming together of the people of God. In the celebration of the Word of God and the eucharistic banquet, the Church is being formed and made visible. The eternal plan of the Father, hidden from all ages, the mystery of Christ, is being made present through human words and gestures - to make what is hidden more real in the life of the visible Church and to hasten the day when the mystery is fully realized and Christ is all in all.

CHRIST AND THE CHURCH

This mystery is a profound one
(Eph. 5:32)

The letter to the Ephesians contains another important use of the word 'mystery'. It comes in chapter 5 at the end of a passage in which Paul speaks of the relationship between husbands and wives in Christ. The mystery that is the eternal plan of God concerns a marriage - the nuptial union between Jesus the Lord and his bride, the Church.

Man and Woman

Towards the end of the teaching on husbands and wives in Eph. 5, Paul quotes a verse from the creation story in Genesis. 'For this reason a man shall leave his father and mother and shall be joined to his wife, and the two shall become one flesh' (Eph. 5:31, citing Gen. 2:24). It is then that

Paul speaks of the 'mystery'. 'This mystery is a profound one, and I am saying that it refers to Christ and the church' (Eph. 5:32).

Is Paul simply making a comparison between the relationship of marriage and that between Christ and the Church? Yes, he is making a comparison, but there seems to be more than an affirmation of similarities. The apostle is making a remarkable statement about the eternal plan of God - which is why he uses the word mystery. From the beginning the creation of man and woman is connected with Christ and the Church. Just as God always has the incarnation of his Son in view in the work of creation ('all things were created for him', that is for the Son, Col. 1:16), so God always has the union of Christ and the Church in view when he creates man and woman.

This teaching on marriage is another example of how from the outset God always has the final end in view. Everything in creation is ordered to the recapitulation of all things in Christ. That means, not just that Jesus is the Saviour who rescues creation and humankind from the effects of sin, but that everything created is to take its rightful place in relation to God's Son 'whom he appointed the heir of all things, through whom also he created the world' (Heb. 1:2).

Israel as Spouse

As with all the other dimensions of the mystery, the revelation concerning Christ and the Church is already being prepared in the Old Testament. In choosing a people as his own, God is acting out of love. So in the song of Moses at the end of Deuteronomy we read, 'For the Lord's portion is his people, Jacob his allotted heritage. He found him in a desert land, and in the howling waste of the wilderness; he encircled him, he cared for him, he kept him as the apple of his eye' (Deut. 32:9-10).

The depth of God's love for his people Israel is particularly shown at the time of their greatest rebellion. This appears quite dramatically in the life of the prophet Hosea. Hosea is told to marry a woman of ill repute. 'The Lord said to Hosea, "Go, take to yourself a wife of harlotry and have children of harlotry, for the land commits great harlotry by forsaking the Lord."' (Hos. 1:2). Hosea is a prophetic figure, not only because he spoke the word of the Lord, but because the Lord made his problematic marriage a prophetic sign. The heart of this prophetic sign is not his marriage, described in chapter 1, but Hosea taking back his wife after her infidelity, described in chapter 3. 'And the Lord said to me, "Go again, love a woman who is beloved of a paramour and is an adulteress; even as the Lord loves the people of Israel, though they turn to other gods and love cakes of raisins"' (Hos. 3:1). By taking back his unfaithful wife, and going way beyond the duty of any husband in Israel, Hosea shows prophetically that the Lord, the God of Israel, will buy back his unfaithful people.

The depiction of the covenant relationship between God and Israel in marital terms occurs typically in the denunciation of their infidelity as adultery. 'Surely, as a faithless wife leaves her husband, so have you been faithless to me, O house of Israel, says the Lord' (Jer. 3:20).[1] This is the word of the Lord, who had said, 'I remember the devotion of your youth, your love as a bride' (Jer. 2:2). In Ezekiel 16, the Lord describes his relationship to Jerusalem in terms of betrothal to a bride: 'When I passed by you again and looked upon you, behold, you were at the age for love; and I spread my skirt over you, and covered your nakedness: yea, I plighted my troth to you and entered into a

covenant with you, says the Lord God, and you
became mine' (Ez. 16:8). But the point of this
description is the denunciation of Jerusalem for her
infidelity: 'Adulterous wife, who receives strangers
instead of her husband!' (Ez. 16:32). The message
is not just one of condemnation, but also one of
promise: 'Yea, thus says the Lord God: I will deal
with you as you have done, who have despised the
oath in breaking the covenant, yet I will remember
my covenant with you in the days of your youth,
and I will establish with you an everlasting
covenant' (Ez. 16:59-60). Through and beyond the
infidelity and the disasters that come upon Judah
and Jerusalem, the Lord reveals the marital
character of the covenant with Israel and his own
extraordinary fidelity.

A passage in the second part of Isaiah captures,
perhaps more than any other, all the movements of
the Lord's heart concerning his beloved and errant
people:

> Fear not, for you will not be ashamed;
>   be not confounded, for you will not be put to
>   shame;
> for you will forget the shame of your youth,
>   and the reproach of your widowhood you will

remember no more.
For your Maker is your husband,
  the Lord of hosts is his name;
and the Holy One of Israel is your Redeemer,
  the God of the whole earth he is called.
For the Lord has called you
  like a wife forsaken and grieved in spirit
like a wife of youth when she is cast off,
  says your God.
For a brief moment I forsook you,
  but with great compassion I will gather you.
In overflowing wrath for a moment
  I hid my face from you,
but with everlasting love I will have compassion
  on you,
says the Lord, your Redeemer.   (Is. 54:4-8)

One book in the Old Testament is all about marriage, the Song of Songs. Some biblical scholars interpret the Song of Songs as simply a celebration of marriage, particularly as it contains no reference to God. But it is not surprising in the light of the prophetic teaching on Israel as bride of the Lord that Jewish teachers of later centuries, both before and after Jesus, understood the Song of Songs in terms of this spousal love of the Lord for Israel. An important element is the desire of the bride and the groom for each other: 'Upon my bed by night, I sought him whom my soul loves' (Song 3:1). 'I slept, but my heart was awake. Hark! my beloved is knocking. "Open to me, my sister, my love, my dove, my perfect one"' (Song 5:2). In this way, the Song of Songs contributed, among both Jews and Christians, to awakening the people's desire for the Lord and their longing for his coming.

Jesus as the Bridegroom

From an early stage of his public ministry, Jesus describes himself as a bridegroom. Probably the first of these occasions is when critics compare the disciples of Jesus unfavourably with the disciples of John the Baptist. Why, the critics complain to Jesus, do your disciples not fast like those of John? Jesus replies, 'Can the wedding guests fast while the bridegroom is still with them? As long as they have the bridegroom with them, they cannot fast. The days will come, when the bridegroom is taken away from them, and then they will fast in that day' (Mark 2:19).[2]

While Jesus does not mention the bride, he compares the disciples to wedding guests. As the

Jews fast to hasten the coming of the Messiah and his kingdom, there is here an implicit claim of Jesus to be the Messiah. It is inappropriate to fast for the Messiah's coming when he is already here. This is a first allusion to two comings of the Messiah. For the Messiah, who is already here, will be taken away, and then it will be appropriate for his disciples to fast - in order to hasten his return. The disciples must have sensed the amazing boldness of Jesus in speaking of himself as the bridegroom. For, as we have seen, the bridegroom in the Old Testament is God himself. So this is an implicit claim not only to be the Messiah, but to be more than the Messiah.

There is also a description of Jesus as the bridegroom in John's Gospel, but here it comes from the mouth of John the Baptist. The Baptist insists that he is not 'the Christ' but has 'been sent before him'. 'He who has the bride is the bridegroom; the friend of the bridegroom, who stands and hears him, rejoices greatly at the bridegroom's voice; therefore this joy of mine is now full' (John 3:29). John the Baptist presents himself as the friend of the bridegroom, who rejoices to hear the bridegroom's voice; but the words of the bridegroom are above all for the bride.

The other Gospel references to Jesus as the bridegroom are found in the context of waiting for his return. In Luke, Jesus urges the disciples to 'be like men who are waiting for their master to come home from the marriage feast, so that they may open to him at once when he comes and knocks' (Luke 12:36). This is similar to the parable of the ten virgins, 'who took their lamps and went to meet the bridegroom' (Matt. 25:1). The focus here is on having oil for their lamps (oil can be understood to refer to the Holy Spirit) and on being alert for the return of the groom.

In Matt. 22, Jesus compares the kingdom of heaven to 'a king who gave a marriage feast for his son' (Matt. 22:2). The clear implication is that the son is Jesus and the king is his heavenly Father. In this case 'the wedding is ready' and everything is prepared; the delay concerns the response of those invited to the celebration.

Between the Old Testament prophets and the teaching of Jesus, we see at least two important developments in the use of this marriage imagery. Whereas in the Old Testament God is the bridegroom, in the Gospels it is Jesus. Whereas in the Old Testament Israel is already the spouse of the Lord, in the Gospels the references to the marriage feast have a strong eschatological 'end-times' character. That is to say, though Jesus is already the bridegroom, the marriage feast takes place at the end and is associated with his second coming. It is from this background that we can now turn to the teaching of the apostle Paul in Ephesians.

The Great Mystery

In Eph. 5:21-6:9, Paul gives a teaching on household relationships: on the relations between husband and wife, between parents and children, and between masters and slaves. All these relationships are seen and presented 'in Christ'. But this practical conclusion to the epistle should not be separated from the doctrinal teaching given in the earlier chapters. Paul treats these relationships 'in Christ', making his teaching more than mere moral exhortation. Household relationships form part of God's plan for all creation, centred on Jesus and now being realized through the Church.

The teaching on husbands and wives is turned into a teaching on Christ and the Church. We see this especially from verse 25: 'Husbands, love your wives, as Christ loved the church and gave himself up for her, that he might sanctify her, having cleansed her by the washing of water with the word, that he might present the church to himself in splendour, without spot or wrinkle or any such thing, that she might be holy and without blemish' (Eph. 5:25-27). The comparison with marriage especially concerns the love of the husband, in this passage mentioned four times.[3] Obviously Paul does not think that the husband literally bathes his wife; the phrase 'the washing of water with the word' is an evident reference to the cleansing of baptism.

At first sight, this passage seems to be an affirmation of the present relationship between Christ and the Church, that is to say, the Church is already fully the wife. But verses 26-27, with the emphasis on the cleansing of the bride 'that he [Christ] might present the church to himself in splendour ... and without blemish', may point rather to the final completion of the Church and the completion of the work of sanctification by Christ's return. Paul would not have forgotten the other 'future completion' passages in Ephesians, notably in chapter 1[4] and chapter 4.[5] So, this passage in Eph. 5 may not be presenting the nuptial union between Christ and the Church as already fully 'realized', in contrast to the wedding feast of the Lamb in the book of Revelation, which happens at the consummation. Paul may have had the Jewish practice of solemn betrothal in mind, so that Ephesians 5 would be presenting the Church as the bride being prepared for her presentation in the perfection of her beauty.

The image of the bridal Church that needs to be cleansed reminds us of the place of repentance and purification in the preparation for the wedding-feast of the Lamb. The recent call of Pope John Paul II for a repentance for past sins of Catholics by the sons and daughters of the Church was made in the context of the preparation of the Church for the new millennium. But this unprecedented papal summons opens the door for Catholics to approach the preparation for the wedding feast of the Lamb with an awareness of the necessity for a corporate purification of all in the life of the Church that cannot pass over into the total purity of the heavenly nuptials.

We should not think of this as a totally different teaching from the mystery of Israel[6] and the mystery of Christ that is the union of Jew and Gentile in the one body.[7] Paul would have been very aware that this bridal Church being prepared for her bridegroom is the Church of which he had spoken in chapter 2. After all, the church of Ephesus, to whom he gives this teaching about marriage, is a church made up of Jewish and Gentile believers which perhaps inspired him to give this teaching on the one 'mystery of Christ', in which the Gentiles are fellow heirs, co-members and co-sharers in the promise.

Mary and the Bride

Catholic theology and devotion sees in Mary, the mother of Jesus, a personal embodiment of the bride. She is the first realization of what is to characterize the whole Church as bride.

In the New Testament, the first intimation of this blessedness of Mary is shown in the greeting of the archangel Gabriel: 'Hail, O favoured one, the Lord is with you' (Luke 1:28). This translation captures the sense that this is like a new name: the One who is favoured. In Greek it is one word, *kecharitōménē*,

more normally translated as 'full of grace'. This is
like a prefiguring of the bride of the Lord, who is to
be 'holy and without blemish' (Eph. 5:27) and to be
clothed with 'the righteous deeds of the saints' (Rev.
19:8).

There is a further hint in the prophecy of Simeon to
Mary in Luke 2:34-35. Simeon speaks first of the
child Jesus: 'Behold, this child is set for the fall and
the rising of many in Israel, and for a sign that is
spoken against'. But then he says to Mary, 'and a
sword will pierce through your own soul also'.
Mary is to be closely linked with the fate of her son.
He will suffer in the body, and thus in his whole
being - and Mary will suffer in her soul.

When Jesus later addresses his mother as 'Woman',
it is an indication that she is playing a
representative role. On these two occasions she is
not just a mother proud of her son at Cana and
grieving over his crucifixion at Calvary.[8] Her
suffering is closely related to the people of Israel.
She suffers, not just as a grieving mother, but as
one who laments over all who 'fall' in Israel, as
Simeon had predicted. In this, Mary is identified
with the suffering 'daughter of Sion' so poignantly
described in the book of Lamentations. In these

references to Mary, there is a discreet evocation of Israel as spouse and of Jerusalem as suffering mother. When the Catholic liturgy applies to Mary the verse from Lamentations, 'Look and see if there is any sorrow like my sorrow' (1:12), it is again not just the sorrow of a mother for her son, but the lament of faithful Israel over unfaithful Israel (and Jerusalem) for the sorrow 'which the Lord inflicted on the day of his fierce anger' (Lam. 1:12). As we shall see, this links up with the vision of the woman in Revelation.[9]

The Wedding Feast of the Lamb

At the end of the visions of John, the seer of Patmos, recorded in the book of Revelation, there are further references to the bride of Jesus. First, there is a mighty sound in heaven, and the cry is heard,

> Hallelujah! For the Lord our God the Almighty reigns.
> Let us rejoice and exult and give him the glory,
> for the marriage of the Lamb has come,
> and his Bride has made herself ready;
> it was granted her to be clothed with fine linen,
> bright and pure

(for the fine linen is the righteous deeds of the
saints). (Rev. 19:6-8)

The reference to the bridegroom as the Lamb
reminds us of an earlier vision of John, where he
sees 'a Lamb standing, as though it had been slain'
and the crowd cries out, 'Worthy is the Lamb who
was slain, to receive power and wealth and wisdom
and might and honour and glory and blessing!'
(Rev. 5:6,12). The redeemer-victor of Calvary is the
bridegroom at the wedding feast. The bride has
been won at the cost of his blood.

The message that 'the marriage of the Lamb has
come' includes the completion of the preparation of
the bride. The imagery of preparation focuses
attention on the beauty of the bride. Esther was
prepared for King Ahasuerus over twelve months:
'six months with oil of myrrh and six months with
spices and ointments' (Esther 2:12). In the spirit
this corresponds to the removal of every spot and
wrinkle from the bride's appearance and refers to
the perfection of her character. We are reminded of
the passage already cited from Eph. 5 in which the
Church is presented 'without spot or wrinkle or any
such thing, that she might be holy and without
blemish' (5:27). The bodily preparation is followed

by clothing and ornamentation. 'The princess is decked in her chamber with gold-woven robes; in many-coloured robes she is led to the king' (Ps. 45:13-14). The robes are the vesture of holiness and righteousness. The 'fine linen, bright and pure' with which the bride is clothed 'is the righteous deeds of the saints' (Rev. 19:8).

The language of preparation also focuses on the longing of both bride and bridegroom for their marital union. Longing is one of the dominant themes in the Song of Songs. It is a longing for the lasting intimacy of which the nearest earthly symbol is that of married love. So in her longing the Church cries out 'Marana tha!' - 'Come, Lord Jesus' (1 Cor. 16:22; Rev. 22:20). This is the cry the Spirit imparts to the Church.

In John's final vision of a new heaven and a new earth (Rev. 21:1), he sees 'the holy city, new Jerusalem, coming down out of heaven from God, prepared as a bride adorned for her husband' (Rev. 21:2). This is repeated a few verses later at the invitation of an angel: 'Come, I will show you the Bride, the wife of the Lamb' (Rev. 21:9).

The identification of the bride with the new

Jerusalem evokes the Old Testament presentation of Jerusalem as the bride or spouse of the Lord. Does this mean that the Old Testament promises concerning the earthly Jerusalem are now totally transferred to the heavenly city? Not entirely, for the second new element in Rev. 21 is the descent of the bride, the holy city, from heaven. With the descent of the heavenly Jerusalem and the coming of the Messiah in glory there will be a coming together of the heavenly and the earthly cities. How this can happen and what this coming together will look like we cannot now imagine. But it fits with the consistent New Testament vision of salvation in which God is at work to deliver the whole creation from the effects of sin and death. As Paul says, 'the creation itself will be set free from its bondage to decay and obtain the glorious liberty of the children of God' (Rom. 8:21). This image of the descent of the heavenly Jerusalem to earth brings together the vision of the Old Testament prophets for a future fulfilment on this earth and the apocalyptic mystical imagery of a heavenly kingdom around the glorified Christ. This understanding also accords well with the imagery of the 'new heavens and new earth' prophesied in Isaiah and in 2 Peter.[10]

Part IV

The Mystery Within

REVEALED BY THE HOLY SPIRIT

He will take what is mine and declare it to you (John 16:14)

We have looked at several significant dimensions of the secret of God, hidden from all ages in the Father's heart, but now revealed in and through his beloved Son. It is now an appropriate moment to focus on the role of the Holy Spirit. The aspects of this secret or mystery already considered have concentrated on the person and mission of Jesus, the Messiah of Israel, the Lord of all peoples and all creation. We have looked at the manifestation of Christ in the flesh (Ch. 3), the plan to gather all things under the authority of Jesus (Ch. 4), the deeper revelation of the cross and the person of Jesus (Ch. 5), the place of the Jewish people in this plan (Ch. 6), the union of Jew and Gentile in the one body of Christ (Ch. 7), the celebration of the mysteries of Christ in the Church (Ch. 8), and the wedding feast of the Lamb, the union of Jesus and his bride (Ch. 9).

All of these dimensions were foreshadowed in the Old Testament. None of them can be arrived at simply by human reasoning and intelligence. They can only be known by the revealing work of the Holy Spirit. The word used in the New Testament for this revelation by the Spirit is *apokalypsis*, which literally means 'unveiling'. The Holy Spirit unveils the mystery, the secret of the Father's heart.

The first passage where Paul mentions mystery is in 1 Corinthians: 'But we impart a secret and hidden wisdom of God, which God decreed before the ages for our glorification' (1 Cor. 2:7). The Greek actually has 'God's wisdom in mystery' (*theou sophían en mystērío*). This 'impartation' comes from the Holy Spirit: 'What no eye has seen, nor ear heard, nor the heart of man conceived, what God has prepared for those who love him, God has revealed to us through the Spirit' (1 Cor. 2:9-10). Paul explains this further: 'No one comprehends the thoughts of God except the Spirit of God' (1 Cor. 2:11). Only the Holy Spirit can make known to us the mystery of Christ, that is the deepest thought of the Father, his one Word - we might say his one thought - from all eternity.

Revealed to Apostles, Prophets and Saints

To whom is the mystery revealed by the Holy Spirit? In Ephesians, the mystery has been 'revealed to his holy apostles and prophets' (3:5). In Colossians, 'the mystery hidden for ages and generations ... [is] now made manifest to his saints' (1:26); 'To them [the saints] God chose to make known how great among the Gentiles are the riches of the glory of this mystery' (Col. 1:27). Who are these holy apostles and prophets? Who are these saints?

Apostles. The foundational testimony was to the resurrection of Jesus from the dead. This was a major criterion for the selection of a new apostle to replace Judas; he 'must become with us a witness to his resurrection' (Acts 1:22). The resurrection appearances are themselves a form of revelation, for all who saw the risen Jesus were believers. So the apostles who form the foundation are the witnesses to the earthly ministry of Jesus and to his resurrection. They clearly include the twelve (with Matthias replacing Judas), who form the twelve foundations of the holy city in Rev. 21:14. But Paul (Gal. 1:1; Eph. 1:1) and James, the brother of the Lord and leader of the church of Jerusalem (Gal. 1:19) are also called apostles. The list Paul gives in 1 Corinthians of those who saw the risen Lord refers to 'all the apostles', who are seemingly not just 'the twelve' plus Paul: 'He appeared to Cephas, then to the twelve. Then he appeared to more than five hundred at one time, most of whom are still alive, though some have fallen asleep. Then he appeared to James, then to all the apostles. Last of all, as to one untimely born, he appeared also to me' (1 Cor. 15:5-8).

Prophets. Who are the prophets to whom the revelation of the Spirit is given? Paul is not referring to the Old Testament prophets, because Ephesians speaks of the revelation of the 'mystery of Christ ... now' (3:4-5). He must be referring to Christian believers, who were recognized by the church community as having the calling of prophet. Later in Ephesians, Paul lists a number of ministries that 'equip the saints ... for building up the body of Christ' (Eph. 4:12). In this list, prophet follows immediately after apostle (Eph. 4:11). In the Acts of the Apostles we find mention of some of these prophets: first, the group of 'prophets and teachers' in Antioch (Acts 13:1), to whom the Holy Spirit gives instructions about the missionary call of Barnabas and Paul. Second, there is mention of a prophet named Agabus, seemingly from Jerusalem, who prophesied 'a great famine' (Acts 11:28) and later foretold Paul's arrest (Acts 21:10-11). Third, Judas and Silas, described as 'leading men among the brethren' (Acts 15:22) are also called prophets (Acts 15:32). In the book of Revelation, those rewarded are 'thy servants, the prophets and saints' (Rev. 11:18) and then the 'saints and apostles and prophets' are called to rejoice over the downfall of the great city, Babylon (Rev. 18:20).

The inclusion of prophets with apostles in this foundational role is a recognition that the work of the Holy Spirit in unveiling the 'mystery of the gospel' (Eph. 6:19) and the 'mystery of our religion' (1 Tim. 3:16) is not limited to the witnesses to the resurrection of Jesus. The church leadership, including Paul, recognized that particular believers were given profound insights into the purposes of the Most High. It was a recognition that the Holy Spirit had given them visions and messages for the Church. Luke may have seen these prophets as having the same gifting as Zechariah, the father of John the Baptist, who 'was filled with the Holy Spirit, and prophesied' (Luke 1:67).

Saints. Lastly, who are the recipients of the revelation described in Colossians as 'his saints' (Col. 1: 26)? The verb used to describe the work of the Spirit here is 'manifest' (*ephanerōthē*). Because this word has a public character, it means we are not just speaking of what Catholics call 'private revelation'. So the 'five hundred' who saw the risen Jesus at the same time (1 Cor. 15:6), and 'the three thousand souls' who witnessed the events of Pentecost and believed (Acts 2:41) all experienced a public manifestation. If this is right, 'his saints' in Col. 1:26 may have a particular reference to the original Jewish believers in Jesus. It does seem that in the New Testament the term 'saints' was first used in a distinctive way for the Jewish believers in Jerusalem and Judea. This is clearly the case in Eph. 2:19, where the Gentile converts are told: 'you are no longer strangers and sojourners [see Eph. 2:12], but you are fellow

citizens with the saints and members of the
household of God, built upon the foundation of the
apostles and prophets, Christ Jesus himself being
the cornerstone' (2:19-20). We see this also in the
references to the collection organized by Paul for
the believers in Jerusalem and in Judea which
speak of 'aid for the saints' (Rom. 15:25); 'the
contribution for the saints' (1 Cor. 16:1), 'the relief
of the saints' (2 Cor. 8:4), 'the offering for the saints'
(2 Cor. 9:1), and 'the wants of the saints' (2 Cor.
9:12).

These reflections point to the revelation to the
'apostles, prophets and saints' having a
foundational character that underpins the reception
of the gospel and the mystery by subsequent
generations of believers, who in their turn are also
called 'saints'[1] and those 'called to be saints' (1 Cor.
1:2).

The Simplicity of Revelation

God reveals the deep things of his heart. As we
have seen, this is supremely the revelation of his
Son. God has placed in our hearts a desire for
depth. We enjoy having secrets. We enjoy having
the secret confidences of others revealed to us.

Most religions have the idea of deep things that are only made known to the privileged few. This is what is meant by the word 'esoteric'. At the time of Jesus, there were in the surrounding world several religions that emphasized a hidden knowledge, or gnosis. Initiates often had to go through complex rites and ceremonies as part of the process of admission to this knowledge. There could be many stages of probation and testing before final admission to the privileged elite.

The revelation of God's secret is nothing like that. It is very simple. It does not involve a long and complicated process requiring a form of technical education. The secret of God's heart is made known by the Holy Spirit. As we see on the Day of Pentecost, the good news of the resurrection of Jesus is proclaimed, and the coming of the kingdom of God. The hearers are told to repent and be baptized: they will receive the forgiveness of sins, and the gift of the Holy Spirit (Acts 2:38). The message is for all. The gift is for those who respond to the grace in the message. The gift of the Holy Spirit is necessary to penetrate the meaning of the message and the new life received.

The simplicity of revelation is the simplicity of
Christian faith. Faith is believing what God has
revealed through the power of the revealing Spirit.
So Paul writes to the Thessalonians: 'we also thank
God constantly for this, that when you received the
word of God which you heard from us, you accepted
it not as the word of men but as what it really is,
the word of God, which is at work in you believers'
(1 Thess. 2:13). This is why faith has an absolute
certainty, a certainty that comes from God and that
cannot be provided by human reasoning.[2]

Entering into the Prophetic

Unlike the Old Testament, where only certain
Israelites were chosen out to be prophets, in the
new covenant established in Jesus, the Holy Spirit
is poured out on all believers. Because all
Christians are promised the gift of the Holy Spirit,
we are all given a share in the prophetic spirit. The
Second Vatican Council teaches that 'The holy
people of God shares also in Christ's prophetic
office'.[3] For the Council this prophetic gifting of the
whole people of God is especially manifested in the
sensus fidelium [the sense of the faithful], in 'the
supernatural appreciation of the faith ... aroused
and sustained by the Spirit of truth'.[4] In the *sensus*

fidelium, the Holy Spirit has brought the Christian revelation alive in the hearts and minds of the Christian faithful. So the mystery revealed by the Spirit at the beginning is always being revealed afresh by the same Spirit to each new generation of Christians.

The whole Church together with every Christian is called to be prophetic with a faith-knowledge coming from the illumination of the Holy Spirit. Such a revealed faith-knowledge embraces the whole mystery of Christ in all its richness. It is not being judgemental but simply realistic to recognize that many Christians have not entered deeply into the heart of the Father revealed in his Son. This is partly because many churchgoers do not really have a living relationship to Jesus Christ. As has been said many times in recent years, they have been 'sacramentalized' but not evangelized. But also many sincere Christians who do have a living faith in Jesus have not advanced on this journey from gospel into mystery.

The spiritual renewal of the Church is addressing both these weaknesses. Only as we grasp the role of the Holy Spirit in the whole mystery of Christ will we be able to receive the full revelation of the

Father into our hearts. This process is expressed most clearly in the words of Jesus about the Holy Spirit: 'When the Spirit of truth comes, he will guide you into all the truth; for he will not speak on his own authority, but whatever he hears he will speak, and he will declare to you the things that are to come. He will glorify me, for he will take what is mine and declare it to you. All that the Father has is mine; therefore I said that he will take what is mine and declare it to you' (John 16:13-15).

The Holy Spirit takes 'what is mine', that is, everything that concerns Jesus, and makes it known in the Church. The Spirit is not an independent agent. The Holy Spirit 'speaks' what he 'hears'. The Holy Spirit takes the Word of God, the personal Word, that is Jesus Christ, and the written testimonial word, that is the Bible, and brings all to living reality within the church community. As we have seen, this includes who Jesus is, his coming in the flesh, his place and role in the Father's purpose, the centrality of his passion, death, and resurrection-ascension, his relationship to his own people and to all the peoples of the earth. As this passage in John makes clear, the Spirit also reveals 'the things that are to come'. This is the goal of all prophecy. It is declaring the mind of God regarding past, present and future. Because the plan of God is directed towards a future fulfilment, the declaring of 'the things that are to come' is essential in the prophetic task of the Church. This is not primarily a matter of predicting future events, though it may often include an element of future prediction. 'The things that are to come' mean above all the coming of the Lord Jesus in glory, the judgement of the living and of the dead, the placing of all things under the rule of Jesus and the establishment of the new heavens and the new earth.

For this task, the Holy Spirit raises up Christians with prophetic gifts. This is a sharing in the prophetic ministry of Jesus that he has poured out on the Church, his body. It is a gift that belongs to the head of the body and is for the sake of the body. The prophet is given a share in God's mind and understanding. The prophet is in some way admitted to 'the council of the Lord', for the prophet Jeremiah mocked the false prophets: 'For whom among them has stood in the council of the Lord to perceive and to hear his word' (Jer. 23:18). Those

called to a prophetic service spend time with the
Lord. They spend time allowing the Holy Spirit to
shed light on God's Word. Prophetic gifts are
poured out for the upbuilding of the whole body of
Christ: 'He who prophesies speaks to men for their
upbuilding and encouragement and consolation' (1
Cor. 14:3). In the context of the Catholic Church,
we can see how, in the new ecclesial movements
and in a particular way in charismatic renewal,
prophetic gifts develop within communities of faith
that feed on the Word. Such gifts are to enable the
whole Church to enter into its prophetic calling,
and to be a herald of 'the things that are to come'.

Thy testimonies are wonderful;
    therefore my soul keeps them.
The unfolding of thy words gives light;
    it imparts understanding to the simple.
With open mouth I pant,
    because I long for thy commandments.

(Ps. 119:129-131)

THE INDWELLING SPIRIT

Christ in you, the hope of glory (Col. 1:27)

Earlier chapters have examined the 'mystery of Christ' that unfolds publicly in human history with the coming of Jesus, the Messiah of Israel. The last chapter presented the role of the Holy Spirit in revealing or unveiling this secret of the Father. This chapter continues to focus on the Holy Spirit as we reflect on the inner or interior dimension of the mystery. This inner work is essential for a full understanding of God's purposes and how God will bring his plan to fruition.

The passage that treats most clearly of the interior dimension of the mystery of Christ is found towards the end of the first chapter of Paul's letter to the Colossians. Paul has spoken of his particular calling 'to make the word of God fully known, the

mystery hidden for ages and for generations but
now made manifest to his saints' (Col. 1:25-26). He
explains the content of the mystery: 'To them God
chose to make known how great among the Gentiles
are the riches of the glory of this mystery, which is
Christ in you, the hope of glory' (Col. 1:27).

While this passage introduces a further dimension
of the mystery, we should note how it fits fully with
all the rich teaching in Ephesians. For the mystery
involves the coming to the Gentiles of 'the riches of
his glory' (Eph. 3:16) which prepares the bride for
her bridegroom, the Messiah of Israel. So it would
be wrong to use this passage in Colossians to
emphasize the indwelling aspect at the expense of
all that is taught on the mystery in Ephesians.

Christ in the Body of Believers

The mystery is here described as 'Christ in you, the
hope of glory'. We may miss in the English
translation that the 'you' is plural: Paul writes,
'Christ in you' (*Christòs en hymin*). The plural does
not weaken the reference to the interior character
of the presence of Jesus in the Christian. But it
does mean that we must avoid turning this
presence into something merely 'individual' or

'personal' in a private sense. The presence of Jesus in us cannot be separated from his presence in others, his presence in our relationships, and his presence in the church community.

Through his Spirit Jesus lives in each Christian. This indwelling presence is above all his dwelling within the Christian community. It is not to be understood separately from the presence promised by Jesus to his disciples when they come together in his name: 'For where two or three are gathered in my name, there am I in the midst of them' (Matt. 18:20). The awareness of the presence of Jesus in and among Christians is found especially in times of prayer and worship together. For gathering 'in his name' means gathering as sons and daughters of the Father, who honour and worship the Father in the name of Jesus.

Of course, we come together in the name of the Lord above all for the celebration of the Eucharist. In the Eucharist we are gathered 'in the name of the Father, and of the Son and of the Holy Spirit' to hear the word of the Lord and to celebrate the memorial of the Lord's saving death. It is the most solemn act of the Christian community. As we feed on the word and feast on the body and blood of the

Lord, we are more deeply formed in Christ and his presence in us is strengthened. At the kiss of peace, we bless each other with the presence of Christ: 'Peace be with you'. The pax has no meaning apart from the presence of Jesus in us and in the community.

However, it would seem that many who go to Mass regularly do not have a strong sense of the presence of the Lord in the worshipping community. Without becoming judgemental of individuals, we need to ask why this is. One factor is the privatized view of faith and our relationship to God that has characterized much of Western Christianity in recent times. In this view, faith is a purely private affair between each individual and God. People who think like this experience the kiss of peace as an intrusion on their prayer or as an irrelevance. Another factor can be a lack of faith-conviction in people whose Mass attendance has become merely formal. In this case, they do not have any sense of the presence of Jesus in them or in others, simply because they do not have any sense of the living God. But there are some, perhaps many, at Mass who do have a sense of God's presence, but they have never been trained or

helped to experience the holy fellowship (the holy
communion) with others in Christ that is the
deepest reality of the Church.

For many, the experience of informal prayer with
others can be a schooling in the presence of the
Lord, whether or not it takes place regularly in a
prayer group. As we pray with other Christians
and as we hear them express in their words of
worship and prayer the faith that is deep within
them, we recognize the presence of the Holy Spirit
in them. We can also recognize this presence in
truly godly behaviour, but it is in the spoken
prayers that come from the depths of the heart that
Christians bear clear witness to the Spirit's
presence within. Such informal prayer together can
develop a sense of the Lord's presence in the group,
and this can make us more aware of his presence in
the gathered Church at Mass.

The Hope of Glory

The presence of the Holy Spirit is the guarantee of
the glory to come. God is preparing us for the
resurrection when 'what is mortal may be
swallowed up by life' and 'for this ... God ... has
given us the Spirit as a guarantee' (2 Cor. 5:4-5).

To be 'a partaker of the Holy Spirit' is to taste 'the goodness of the word of God and the powers of the age to come' (Heb. 6:4-5).

So when Paul tells the Colossians that the mystery is 'Christ in you, the hope of glory', he is saying that the church community contains her future hope within her own life. Again this is primarily a communal reality, a promise to the community. Christ dwelling in the church community provides the hope for the communal shared glory of the resurrection. For the hope to be a living hope for the Church, Christ in the church community has in some way to be an experienced reality.

Why is this hope the hope of glory? The Jesus who is present in the church community is the risen Lord Jesus. He cannot be present without his glory. Because Jesus is present in a hidden way, his glory is present in a hidden way. Paul says: 'And we all, with unveiled faces, beholding the glory of the Lord, are being changed into his likeness from one degree of glory to another; for this comes from the Lord, who is the Spirit' (2 Cor. 3:18). The life of the Spirit in us, though hidden, is a presence of glory, that is preparing us for the coming glory that will no longer be hidden.

From Suffering to Glory

The first Christians quickly found themselves in situations of suffering and persecution. They were comforted by recalling words of Jesus, later gathered in the Gospels, that spoke of the disciples following in the way of their master. 'Remember the word that I said to you, "A servant is not greater than his master." If they persecuted me, they will persecute you' (John 15:20). Jesus promised his disciples the presence and the guidance of the Holy Spirit in times of persecution: 'And when they bring you to trial and deliver you up, do not be anxious beforehand what you are to say; but say whatever is given you in that hour, for it is not you who speak, but the Holy Spirit.' (Mark 13:11). Paul developed this into a teaching on baptism and the Christian life, expressed particularly in Rom. 6: 'For if we have been united with him in a death like his, we shall certainly be united with him in a resurrection like his' (v.5).

In Philippians, Paul returns to the theme of present suffering and the resurrection to come. He prays 'that I may know him and the power of his resurrection, and may share his sufferings, becoming like him in his death, that if possible I may attain the resurrection from the dead' (Phil. 3:10-11). Paul understands his sufferings as an apostle as a sharing in the sufferings of Jesus. But he knows that in the midst of these present sufferings he can know Jesus and the power of his resurrection. So as we are faithful to the Lord Jesus in our sufferings for his sake, we experience even now the power of his resurrection. In this, the Lord is preparing us for the day of our own resurrection.

Paul addresses the theme of present affliction and future glory more directly in Rom. 8. The indwelling Holy Spirit bears witness within us - Paul says 'with our spirit' - 'that we are children of God, and if children, then heirs, heirs of God and fellow heirs with Christ, provided we suffer with him in order that we may also be glorified with him' (Rom. 8: 16-17). We are children of God, we are heirs of Christ, and we suffer. Paul's gaze is on the goal. He sees the glory: 'I consider that the sufferings of this present time are not worth comparing with the glory that is to be revealed to us' (Rom. 8:18).

From Creation to Church

Paul then develops the hope of glory in a surprising way. Extraordinarily, to our way of thinking, he turns to creation before speaking of the Church and the Christian. First, he emphasizes the longing: 'For the creation waits with eager longing for the revealing of the sons of God' (Rom. 8:19). The longing of the whole creation is a consequence of the impact of sin on the world-system. Human sin not only disturbs human relations, it pollutes the air, the land and the sea. The man, Adam, was entrusted with responsibility for the creation in which he was placed: 'Have dominion over the fish of the sea and over the birds of the air and over every living thing that moves upon the earth.' (Gen. 1:28). When man rebels, the creation suffers. The intimate connection of the destinies of the people and of the land is shown many times in the Old Testament. It is shown in Israel's worship: 'The earth is the Lord's and the fullness thereof, the world and those who dwell therein' (Ps. 24:1).[1] It is particularly emphasized by the prophets:[2] 'The earth lies polluted under its inhabitants; for they have transgressed the laws, violated the statutes, broken the everlasting covenant' (Is. 24:5). So 'the creation was subjected to futility, not of its own will but by the will of him who subjected it in hope' (Rom. 8:20). This subjection in hope comes in some way from God the creator, because God alone is the author of hope. The hope of the creation is then specified: 'because the creation itself will be set free from its bondage to decay and obtain the glorious liberty of the children of God' (Rom. 8:21).

The liberation of creation is linked with the redemption of humankind. As human sin introduced the 'bondage to decay' that leads to and accompanies death, so the deliverance of humans from sin and all its effects will lead to the freedom of creation. That is why 'creation waits with eager longing for the revealing of the sons of God' (Rom. 8:19). The resurrection of the dead will 'reveal' the sons (and daughters) of God. We humans will be seen in the glory of Christ, the new Adam.[3] The closeness of the bonds between the creation and humans is so great that the creation will enjoy 'the glorious liberty of the children of God' (Rom. 8:21).

What does it mean for the creation to wait with eager longing? It is hard for us to comprehend. But it must mean that in some way God as creator has placed in every creature and in every part of

his creation an inner ordering towards the destiny
he has purposed from the beginning. When the
creation is unable to enter into its destiny, there is
frustration. Yet this passage also shows that the
suffering and frustration are not in vain. Paul uses
the image of childbirth: 'We know that the whole
creation has been groaning in travail together until
now' (Rom. 8:22). The travail of birth pangs is an
image of hope. The sufferings are not pointless.
They are part of a process that will issue in a birth.
The suffering prepares the way for new life. The
agony of the creation prepares for the birth and the
coming forth of the kingdom.

The Church Groans Inwardly

Paul now moves from the longing and groaning of
the creation to the longing and the groaning of the
Church. 'Christ in you, the hope of glory' leads to a
groaning for the coming forth of the kingdom in all
the glory and the power of Jesus. 'Not only the
creation, but we ourselves, who have the first fruits
of the Spirit, groan inwardly as we wait for
adoption as sons, the redemption of our bodies'
(Rom. 8:23). The context moving from creation to
humans is so strongly corporate and all-embracing

that we should not interpret this verse simply in terms of the individual Christian.

All creation longs and groans for the coming redemption. Does the whole human race so long and groan? Paul does not say so. This is no doubt deliberate. It is the Church that longs and groans, because the longing and groaning in human beings comes from those who have received the life of the Spirit. Through the indwelling Spirit, we can enter into the longing of the Lord, his thirst for the final fulfilment in the world of the work he personally completed on Calvary with the words 'It is finished' (John 19:30).

Why does the longing and the groaning only begin with the gift of the Holy Spirit? The answer is contained in the word 'firstfruits' (*aparchē*) which refer to the beginnings of the harvest, to the firstfruit that is to be consecrated to God. The firstfruits are a sign of the full harvest to come. The gift of the Spirit is already a share in the life of the risen Jesus. The Christian already tastes something of the age to come: the fellowship and communion with the Blessed Trinity, the desire to worship, the thirst for holiness, the desire to evangelize, the love for the poor. All these are

signs of the presence of the Spirit of God. The
Christian who tastes the love of Jesus and the
goodness of eternal life longs for the fullness to
come.

The longing includes an element of groaning.
Groaning suggests a purposeful longing in the
midst of suffering and travail. We taste the
firstfruits of the Spirit in a world of suffering. As
Paul says, 'we have this treasure in earthen vessels'
(2 Cor. 4:7). Some translations have 'vessels of
clay'. The groaning of Christians and of the Church
is directed towards the goal. It is part of a struggle,
a reaching for the future, that requires a waiting.
But though there is an element of suffering, the
groaning is suffused with hope. We groan inwardly
knowing that our adoption as sons and daughters of
the resurrection is certain; and the Spirit's presence
in us is the guarantee of that certainty. Paul
therefore continues: 'For in this hope we were
saved' (Rom. 8:24).

After the groaning of the creation and the groaning
of the Christians, Paul even mentions the groaning
of the Holy Spirit: 'we do not know how to pray as
we ought, but the Spirit himself intercedes for us
with sighs too deep for words' (Rom. 8:26). The

word for 'sighs' here belongs to the same word-group as the words earlier translated as 'groaning'. We do not know how to pray for the coming of the kingdom, or how to pray for the final deliverance. But the Holy Spirit, who does know, comes to our aid. The groaning of the Holy Spirit, the sighs of the Spirit, are very clearly purposeful: they are not just sighs and groans of frustration, but deep urgings of God for the final accomplishment of the Father's plan.

When we pray in the Spirit, when we surrender our praying to the Holy Spirit within us, we allow this divine urging to find expression through our spirits. In this way we are able to pray much vaster prayers than we can formulate or understand. This surrender to the prayer and longing of the Spirit stretches our spirits. It increases the capacity of our hearts. We contribute in some way to God's moving of his purpose towards the climax of the final deliverance. 'The Spirit intercedes for the saints according to the will of God' (Rom. 8:27). 'Lord, come in glory. Lord, come, give us a share in your glory. Come and bring the mystery to its completion.'

Part V

The Consummation

THE LAST TRUMPET

Lo! I tell you a mystery (1 Cor. 15:51)

As we near the end of our reflection on *God's Masterplan*, we must look at a passage that speaks of the end as mystery. It comes in 1 Cor. 15, a chapter completely devoted to the resurrection of the dead: first, the resurrection of Jesus, and then our own resurrection. At the end of a long exposition on the resurrection of the human body, Paul finally speaks about the day of resurrection: 'Lo! I tell you a mystery. We shall not all sleep, but we shall all be changed, in a moment, in the twinkling of an eye, at the last trumpet. For the trumpet will sound, and the dead will be raised imperishable, and we shall be changed' (1 Cor. 15:51-52).

The Resurrection of the Dead

In the first of Paul's letters in the New Testament, we have a teaching on the destiny of the sisters and brothers who have already died. They have 'fallen asleep'. Christians are not to grieve over the dead as unbelievers do 'who have no hope' (1 Thess. 4:13). When the Lord comes in his glory, 'God will bring with him those who have fallen asleep.' (1 Thess. 4:14). There will be those who are still alive on the earth when the Lord comes but, Paul insists, they 'shall not precede those who have fallen asleep' (1 Thess. 4:15). This is the same teaching outlined above: 'We shall not all sleep, but we shall all be changed' (1 Cor. 15:51).

In describing the resurrection of the dead Paul uses the imagery of the *shofar*, the ram's horn, rather misleadingly translated as 'trumpet', which is sounded for the assembly of the Lord's people. 'For the Lord himself will descend from heaven with a cry of command, with the archangel's call, and with the sound of the trumpet of God. And the dead in Christ will rise first' (1 Thess. 4:16). In Jewish exegesis the Day of Judgement will be announced by the blowing of the *shofar*, an understanding

found in Matthew's Gospel, where Jesus says that
the Son of man 'will send out his angels with a loud
trumpet call, and they will gather his elect from the
four winds, from one end of heaven to the other'
(Matt. 24:31).

This teaching on the resurrection of the dead is also
repeated in 1 Corinthians: Jesus is 'the first fruits
of those who have fallen asleep' (1 Cor. 15:20). 'For
as in Adam all die, so also in Christ shall all be
made alive. But each in his own order: Christ the
first fruits, then at his coming those who belong to
Christ' (1 Cor. 15:22-23).

People are sometimes puzzled by Paul's teaching in
1 Thessalonians that 'we who are alive, who are
left, shall be caught up together with them in the
clouds to meet the Lord in the air' (1 Thess. 4:17).
In the Jewish cosmology that Paul shared, the air
refers to the zone between the heavens and the
earth. This intermediate zone was believed to be
under the control of evil spirits, a belief that is
expressed elsewhere in the Pauline letters: 'You
once walked, following the course of this world,
following the prince of the power of the air, the
spirit that is now at work in the sons of
disobedience' (Eph. 2:2). The significance of

meeting Christ 'in the air' would then be the final removal of the power of Satan from the zone between God and the world. In the final consummation, all barriers between God and humankind are destroyed.

Paul does not mention the resurrection of the lost. This teaching is found in the Gospel of John: 'the hour is coming when all who are in the tombs will hear his voice and come forth, those who have done good, to the resurrection of life, and those who have done evil, to the resurrection of judgment' (John 5:28-29). This verse is cited in the *Catechism of the Catholic Church*, which affirms that 'all the dead will rise'.[1]

The Day of Christ Jesus

At the outset of his correspondence with the Christians of Corinth, Paul had told them: 'you are not lacking in any spiritual gift, as you wait for the revealing of our Lord Jesus Christ; who will sustain you to the end, guiltless in the day of our Lord Jesus Christ' (1 Cor. 1:7-8). Paul, who knew the Old Testament so well, takes the prophetic concept of 'the day of the Lord' and transforms it into 'the day of our Lord Jesus Christ'. Equivalent phrases are found in other passages: 'the day of the Lord Jesus' (1 Cor. 5:5; 2 Cor. 1:14); 'the day of Jesus Christ' (Phil. 1:6); 'the day of Christ' (Phil. 1:10; 2:16).[2]

In the Old Testament, 'the day of the Lord' is a day of judgement to be dreaded with great fear. 'Woe to you who desire the day of the Lord! Why would you have the day of the Lord? ... Is not the day of the Lord darkness, and not light, and gloom with no brightness in it?' (Amos 5:18, 20). The same frightening message is found in the prophets Joel and Zephaniah: 'Let all the inhabitants of the land tremble, for the day of the Lord is coming, it is near, a day of darkness and gloom, a day of clouds and thick darkness!' (Joel 2:1-2). 'The great day of the Lord is near, near and hastening fast; the sound of the day of the Lord is bitter, the mighty man cries aloud there. A day of wrath is that day, a day of distress and anguish, a day of ruin and devastation, a day of darkness and gloom, a day of clouds and thick darkness, a day of trumpet blast and battle cry against the fortified cities and against the lofty battlements.' (Zeph. 1:14-16).

The depiction of 'the days of the Son of man' in the synoptic Gospels is in line with the Old Testament prophets. 'And if the Lord had not shortened the days, no human being would be saved; but for the sake of the elect, whom he chose, he shortened the days' (Mark 13:20).[3] But in the New Testament letters, there is a dramatic change of outlook: 'The day of Christ Jesus' is not a day to be feared by the faithful; it is a day to be anticipated with peace and joy. Paul's message to the believers is: 'you are not in darkness, brethren, for that day to surprise you like a thief' (1 Thess 5:4). 'Since we belong to the day, let us be sober, and put on the breastplate of faith and love, and for a helmet the hope of salvation. For God has not destined us for wrath, but to obtain salvation through our Lord Jesus Christ' (1 Thess. 5:8-9). What has happened between the words of Jesus and the teaching of Paul is the day of Calvary, a fulfilment of the 'day of the Lord', when 'there was darkness over the whole earth until the ninth hour' (Luke 23:44). As a result, 'there is now no condemnation for those who are in Christ Jesus' (Rom. 8:1). For those baptized into the death of Jesus, there is to be no anxiety 'as we wait in joyful hope for the coming of our Saviour Jesus Christ',[4] for Jesus has himself experienced the darkness and the wrath.

Vision Face to Face

There are a few passages in the New Testament
that speak of the transformed relationship to God
that will come with the resurrection of the body. In
1 Cor. 13, the famous chapter on love, Paul writes:
'For now we see in a mirror dimly, but then face to
face. Now I know in part; then I shall understand
fully, even as I have been fully understood' (1 Cor.
13:12). Paul is contrasting our present knowledge,
the partial knowledge of faith, with the future
knowledge in the kingdom, the total knowledge of
direct vision.

In the first letter of John, the apostle writes:
'Beloved, we are God's children now; it does not yet
appear what we shall be, but we know that when
he appears we shall be like him, for we shall see
him as he is' (1 John 3:2). We cannot imagine what
the life of the resurrection will be like. It will be
far beyond the capacity of our imaginations, limited
as they are by our earthly horizons. But we, in our
transformed state, will see him, Jesus, in his
transformed state. Relationships in the kingdom of
God will be quite different from what we know now.
They will be totally transparent. The human face

will no longer be a mask as well as a mirror. We will see all, and all will be glorious.

Paul also speaks to the Philippians about this transformation: 'But our commonwealth is in heaven, and from it we await a Saviour, the Lord Jesus Christ, who will change our lowly body to be like his glorious body, by the power which enables him even to subject all things to himself' (Phil. 3:20-21). At the resurrection, we shall become like Jesus in heaven: not just as depicted in the resurrection appearances, but in the full glory of his ascension.

Spiritual Body

In 1 Cor. 15 Paul contrasts the 'sowing' of burial with the 'raising' of the resurrection. 'So it is with the resurrection of the dead. What is sown is perishable, what is raised is imperishable. It is sown in dishonour, it is raised in glory. It is sown in weakness, it is raised in power. It is sown a physical body, it is raised a spiritual body' (1 Cor. 15:42-44).

The resurrection body is spiritual, because in the resurrection there will no longer be any subordination of the soul and the spirit to the body.

In our present human condition, the body is not just servant but also master. This subordination is not only operative when disordered bodily desires lead to greed and lust, but it is also shown by our need for food, drink and sleep.

The process of ageing reveals another aspect of bodily dominance. Yet for the Christian, filled with the Holy Spirit, the process of ageing is not just one of deterioration. Paul expresses the paradox in this way: 'So we do not lose heart. Though our outer nature is wasting away, our inner nature is being renewed every day' (2 Cor. 4:16). As saintly people get older, and their physical powers decline, the disparity between the growing holiness of the inner being and the weakness of the body becomes ever more apparent. We can perhaps remember pictures of Mother Teresa of Calcutta in the frailty of her old age, when the light of God within had become almost transparent. Paul sees the glory that is in preparation: 'For this slight momentary affliction is preparing for us an eternal weight of glory beyond all comparison' (2 Cor. 4:17).

In the spiritual body of the resurrection, the glory of God filling the spirit will flow out and through the whole human body. It is hard for us to imagine this transformation. Jesus pointed to it, when he refuted the objections to the resurrection raised by the Sadducees: 'The sons of this age marry and are given in marriage; but those who are accounted worthy to attain to that age and to the resurrection from the dead neither marry nor are given in marriage, for they cannot die any more, because they are equal to angels and are sons of God, being sons of the resurrection' (Luke 20:34-36). Marriage belongs to the conditions of this age prior to the resurrection, although subsequent to the fall it is also subject to sin and weakness.[5] In our present condition, in which the spirit is in a degree of subordination to the body, bodily union in marriage contributes to the union of soul and spirit. But in the glory of the resurrection, the spirit will suffuse the whole of our bodily existence, and there will be no gap between body and spirit. There will be total communication and total communion.

Total Trinitarian Communion

The perfect fellowship of the kingdom of God that follows the transformation of the resurrection will be our total insertion - spirit, soul and body - into the communion of the most holy Trinity. Through the Holy Spirit, we are united to the incarnate Son to form one body with him as head, so entering into full sonship and daughterhood of the Father. But we must not imagine the divine persons as external to one another. Here again our human models fail and our human imagination is out of its depth. The communion of the kingdom is the total answer to the prayer of Jesus, 'that they may all be one; even as thou, Father, art in me, and I in thee, that they also may be in us' (John 17:21). 'Our fellowship is with the Father and with his Son Jesus Christ' (1 John 1:3). Our total beings in all our graced relationships now enter into this perfect fellowship. The perfect fatherhood of the Father will be shown forth, as will be the Father's gift of the Spirit 'without measure' (John 4:34) that is now demonstrated in the fullness of the body of Christ, head and members.

Our final union with Jesus will involve total acceptance of his authority, which is inseparable from his love, his justice and his mercy. He will be our head and our brother, and there will be no tension between the two. In the totally glorified body of Christ all the redeemed will be filled with all the fullness of God that is in Christ: 'He has put all things under his feet and has made him the head over all things for the church, which is his body, the fullness of him who fills all in all' (Eph. 1:22-23).

There will be total worship of the triune God and total communion with God and with one another. We cannot imagine how these can fully co-exist, though the Eucharist is our deepest earthly preparation for this endless worship and communion. The fullest picture we have of this glory to come is perhaps the vision described by John in Rev. 7. Here he sees first the 144,000 sealed from all the tribes of Israel, followed by the vision of 'a great multitude which no man could number, from every nation, from all tribes and peoples and tongues, standing before the throne and before the Lamb' (Rev. 7:9). They all cry out with a loud voice, 'Salvation belongs to our God who sits upon the throne, and to the Lamb!' (Rev. 7:10). There will be total recognition of all we have received from God in creation and in the redemption through the blood of the Lamb. There will be total delight in our God, who will be totally delighted - finally - with us, his creatures. The mystery will then have reached its completion.

THE MYSTERY OF INIQUITY

*For the mystery of lawlessness is already
at work (2 Thess. 2:7)*

While mystery in the New Testament primarily
refers to the plan of God hidden for all ages and
now manifest in his Son, there are a few references
to a negative mystery. There is a mystery of evil, a
mystery of iniquity.

The writings of Paul and of John each have one
reference to the sinister mystery. Paul tells the
Thessalonians that 'the mystery of lawlessness is
already at work' (2 Thess. 2:7). And in the book of
Revelation, John speaks of 'the mystery of the
woman' (Rev. 17:7), earlier identified as 'Babylon
the great, mother of harlots and of earth's
abominations' (Rev. 17:5).

Why a Mystery of Evil?

Most people enjoy novels and movies in which good
finally triumphs over evil. Typically, the plight of
the righteous becomes desperate and the tables are
only turned at the last minute through the extraordinary ingenuity and courage of the righteous
hero. Yet of course we know all along who is going
to win.

The biblical view of world history is rather unusual.
There is a constant battle between good and evil.
But the decisive battle has already been fought.
Even though the powers of darkness seemingly still
possess great power, they are already condemned to
defeat and destruction. The decisive battle took
place on the cross of Calvary. 'But woe to you, O
earth and sea, for the devil has come down to you
in great wrath, because he knows that his time is
short!' (Rev. 12:12).

Yet while the Scriptures make frequent reference to
the element of conflict and battle,[1] they carefully
avoid any suggestion that there is a conflict
between equal or comparable forces. The principal
adversary, variously described as the devil, Satan
and the serpent, is a creature, not a kind of demi-

god. The *Catechism of the Catholic Church* emphasizes: 'The power of Satan is, nonetheless, not infinite. He is only a creature, powerful from the fact that he is pure spirit, but still a creature.'[2]

While we have to avoid any kind of dualism that seems to place God and the devil on the same level, the biblical narrative, particularly in the New Testament, makes clear that there is super-human opposition to the project of God. In the letter to the Ephesians, Paul speaks of the nature of this opposition: 'For we are not contending against flesh and blood, but against the principalities, against the powers, against the world rulers of this present darkness, against the spiritual hosts of wickedness in the heavenly places' (Eph. 6:12).

It is one of the more bizarre aspects of Christian life today that at a time when the forces of darkness are so conspicuously at work in our world, there are many within the Church who ignore or even deny the character of this opposition. We live at a time when we seem powerless to deal with political and commercial corruption, the arms trade, narco-crime, the AIDS epidemic, ethnic hatred. The Bible and the Church tell us that we are not just faced by human sin and weakness, but by spiritual forces that exploit and reinforce human opposition to God.

The mystery of iniquity reminds us that the outworking of God's plan is not easy. It is not without cost. As Christians, we cannot just sit back, ignore the size of the problems and await the dawn. The opposition to God's kingdom and his righteousness has already cost the blood of the Son of God. Victory for the righteous is assured, but only through inclusion in the cross and resurrection of Jesus. The disciples are active combatants in what Paul calls 'the good fight' (2 Tim. 4:7).

The Opposition of Babylon

Chapters 17 and 18 of the book of Revelation speak of the final overthrow and destruction of the great city called 'Babylon the great'.[3] The 'mystery of the woman' is the culmination of human efforts aided by the powers of darkness to create the counter-city, the city of man, built on military might and economic power, that worships itself rather than the living God. Through biblical history a sharp contrast develops between Jerusalem, the city of God, and Babylon, the city of evil.

Before Babylon became an oppressor of Israel, it signified human pride and opposition to God through the Tower of Babel, the Hebrew name for Babylon. 'Come, let us build ourselves a city, and a tower with its top in the heavens' (Gen. 11:4). When Babylon becomes the instrument of the Lord for the punishment of rebellious Judah (see Jer. 21:3-7), it is punished in turn for its arrogance, cruelty, sorcery and idolatry. 'I will requite Babylon and all the inhabitants of Chaldea before your very eyes for all the evil that they have done in Zion, says the Lord' (Jer. 51:24).

Even though the city of Babylon had been destroyed long before the time of Jesus, it remained a powerful symbol for every project of human exaltation over and against the plan of God. In the first letter of Peter, the name Babylon is given to Rome, the capital of the great empire that spread throughout the Mediterranean basin and beyond.[4] This is also the perspective of John in the book of Revelation. 'Babylon the great' is embodied afresh in pagan Rome. Rome was built on seven hills, so we read that 'the seven heads are seven mountains on which the woman is seated' (Rev. 17: 9).

Babylon is not just ancient Rome. Babylon was embodied in a particular way in pagan Rome. Babylon is the city of corruption, the symbol of every form of human arrogance that oppresses the righteous, that worships power and thirsts for human blood. Every disaster that strikes human empires which oppress the righteous and persecute the saints is a further fulfilment of the biblical warnings against Babylon. When new forms of tyranny arise, their Babylonian character is revealed most clearly in their ruthless elimination of the righteous and in the making of many martyrs. The city of evil once again attacks the Church in its effort to frustrate and thwart the plan of God, the mystery of Christ.

The Importance of the Martyrs

To understand the overthrow of pagan Rome, foretold in Rev. 17-18, we must note the centrality of the Christian martyrs in the battle between the two cities, the city of God and the city of evil. The book of Revelation is a message of consolation to the Church undergoing severe persecution. The 'souls of those who had been slain for the word of God and for the witness they had borne' cry out with a loud voice: 'O Sovereign Lord, holy and true, how long before thou wilt judge and avenge our blood on those who dwell upon the earth?' (Rev. 6:10). They are told to rest a little longer until the number of martyrs would be complete.[5] In the passage in chapter 12, that speaks of the casting down of Satan to the earth, the martyrs are mentioned again: 'they have conquered him by the blood of the Lamb and by the word of their testimony, for they loved not their lives even unto death' (Rev. 12:11).

So, at the beginning of the indictment of the 'woman', who is 'Babylon the great, mother of harlots and of earth's abominations', John says: 'I saw the woman, drunk with the blood of the saints and the blood of the martyrs of Jesus' (Rev. 17:6). The sign of the city's sin is the blood of the saints: 'And in her was found the blood of prophets and of saints, and of all who have been slain on earth' (Rev. 18:24).

In the destruction of Rome-Babylon, described in Rev. 18, reference is made to the mourning and devastation of the kings and the merchants, the power-brokers. The destruction of the city is presented as the vindication of the martyrs: 'Rejoice over her, O heaven, O saints and apostles and prophets, for God has given judgment for you against her' (Rev. 18:20). The great multitude in heaven rejoice and praise the just judgements of God: 'Hallelujah! Salvation and glory and power belong to our God, for his judgments are true and just; he has judged the great harlot who corrupted the earth with her fornication, and he has avenged on her the blood of his servants' (Rev. 19:1-2).

In the twentieth century, there have been more martyrs than in all the previous Christian centuries combined. Pope John Paul II has grasped deeply the significance of the martyrs of our day: 'At the end of the second millennium, the Church has once again become a Church of martyrs.'[6] This is a sharp reminder that the final fulfilment of God's plan, the realization of the mystery, will not come about by gradual moral improvement or steady spiritual advance. There is an intensifying battle between the forces of light and the forces of darkness.

Babylon and Jerusalem

Just as the Scriptures contrast the two cities, Babylon and Jerusalem, so in Revelation there is a contrast between the great harlot of chapter 17 and the woman with child of chapter 12. This chapter also emphasizes the ferocity of the battle. 'And a great portent appeared in heaven, a woman clothed with the sun, with the moon under her feet, and on her head a crown of twelve stars' (Rev. 12:1). This woman 'was with child and she cried out in her pangs of birth, in anguish for delivery' (Rev. 12:2). Immediately there appears a 'great red dragon', later identified with 'that ancient serpent, who is called the Devil and Satan' (Rev. 12:9), who seeks to 'devour her child when she brought it forth' (Rev. 12:4).

Who is this woman? Almost all exegetes agree that the woman is Israel, or more specifically Jerusalem. For the child born of the woman is clearly the Messiah. He is 'to rule all the nations with a rod of iron' (Rev. 12:5), a clear reference to verse 9 of Psalm 2, a Messianic psalm in which the Lord says: 'I have set my king on Zion, my holy hill' (Ps. 2:6). But it would seem wrong to deny any reference to Mary as the mother of Jesus. However, affirming a reference to Mary is not an alternative to Israel and Jerusalem. Rather, a reference to Mary sees her embodying the calling of Israel to bring forth the Messiah of the Lord.

The woman of Rev. 12 expresses the transformation
from Israel before Christ to the Church formed of
Jewish disciples, of whom Mary was the first. The
chapter that begins with the woman crying out in
the pains of childbirth ends with the dragon still
angry with the woman, making 'war on the rest of
her offspring, on those who keep the commandments of God and bear testimony to Jesus' (Rev.
12:17). The battle between the two cities,
Jerusalem and Babylon, symbolized by the two
women, is thus central to Revelation's vision of the
Church.

The Battle of the Last Days

Paul warns the church at Thessalonika against
deception concerning the coming of the Lord. 'Let
no one deceive you in any way; for that day will not
come, unless the rebellion comes first, and the man
of lawlessness is revealed, the son of perdition' (2
Thess. 2:3). Paul adds that there is something
restraining this evil figure. So while 'the mystery
of lawlessness is already at work' (2 Thess. 2:7), it
is only when the restraining factor is removed that
'the lawless one will be revealed' (2 Thess. 2:8). In
Paul's prophetic understanding, this is the final
rebellion, when the Lord Jesus will come: 'and the

Lord Jesus will slay him with the breath of his
mouth and destroy him by his appearing and his
coming' (2 Thess. 2:8).

In the first letter of John, we read about the
'antichrist'. 'Children, it is the last hour; and you
have heard that antichrist is coming, so now many
antichrists have come; therefore we know that it is
the last hour' (1 John 2:18). For John, the
antichrist is 'he who denies the Father and the Son'
(1 John 2:22). The spirit of antichrist will not
confess that Jesus Christ is come in the flesh (see 1
John 4:3; 2 John 7). We will understand John's
teaching on the antichrist better when we recall
that 'Christ' means 'Messiah'. From the first
coming of Messiah Jesus to the second, there are
those who oppose his message and obstruct his
mission. For John, these opponents of the Messiah
are the antichrist. As the Messianic hope of Israel
will only be completely fulfilled at the second
coming of the Lord, so the opposition to the Messiah
grows as his day approaches. For John, it was
already the 'last hour' (1 John 2:18) because the
Messiah had come in the flesh.

In 2 Thessalonians, the hallmark of the 'man of
lawlessness' is that he 'opposes and exalts himself

against every so-called god or object of worship, so that he takes his seat in the temple of God, proclaiming himself to be God' (2 Thess. 2:4). No doubt, the Jews of Paul's day would have seen King Antiochus Epiphanes, who desecrated the temple in Jerusalem in the second century BCE, as a forerunner of the 'man of lawlessness'. But it is only in the twentieth century that systematic atheism appeared and with it the most ruthless and systematic persecutions against Judaism and Christianity. Only in the modern world has there grown up a systematic attempt to build a society without God, in which morality is totally a human construction and freedom includes freedom from all religious restraint.

This is not to say that there have been no positive developments in modern times. The conflict between good and evil was obscured at certain times in the past by the Church's failure to distinguish between the authentically human and the customs of feudal and patriarchal societies. The tragedy of the Enlightenment struggles of the eighteenth and nineteenth centuries is that the Church fought for too long to defend what was contingent and inessential as well as defending the law of God and the revelation of Christ. The twentieth century renewal of the Catholic Church has involved the struggle to separate what needed to be abandoned from the core-tradition that needed to be preserved and retrieved. But it is precisely as the Church is renewed that the attacks against the Church become more intense and more violent. For the works of darkness are directed against the coming of the kingdom. They are anti-Christ, anti-Messianic, anti-kingdom.

It is appropriate to close this chapter with a citation from the *Catechism of the Catholic Church* that mentions 'The mystery of iniquity'. This comes in its section 'From thence he will come again to judge the living and the dead'. Here the *Catechism* speaks of the Church's ultimate trial: 'Before Christ's second coming the Church must pass through a final trial that will shake the faith of many believers. The persecution that accompanies her pilgrimage on earth will unveil the "mystery of iniquity" in the form of a religious deception offering men an apparent solution to their problems at the price of apostasy from the truth.'[7] It continues: 'The Church will enter the glory of the kingdom only through this final Passover, when she will follow her Lord in his death and Resurrection. The kingdom will be fulfilled, then, not by a historic triumph of the Church through a progressive ascendancy, but only by God's victory over the final unleashing of evil, which will cause his Bride to come down from heaven.'[8]

EPILOGUE

This book has examined the biblical use of the term 'mystery'. As we have seen, the mystery is supremely the 'mystery of Christ', the eternal plan of the Father hidden for all ages, but now made manifest in Christ and revealed by the Holy Spirit to his holy ones.

I have suggested that even where the use of the word 'mystery' in the New Testament does not explicitly refer to the plan of God now being revealed in Christ, it still retains these connotations. There is a harmony and unity among all the references to the mystery in Paul from Romans onwards - the only exception being the reference to 'the mystery of lawlessness' in 2 Thessalonians, an early letter written before Paul began to teach about the eternal plan of God as mystery.

The mystery is first the mystery of Jesus Christ himself, the Word made flesh. Jesus, the incarnate Son of God, is central to the Father's plan to 'unite all things in him, things in heaven and things on earth' (Eph. 1:10). The fuller revelation of God's plan in turn deepens our knowledge of Jesus himself, 'in whom are hid all the treasures of wisdom and knowledge' (Col. 2:3). The place of Israel in this plan also forms part of the secret of the Father who, even as he unites Gentile and Jew in the one body of Messiah, does not reject his chosen people. They will receive mercy just as the Gentiles have received mercy. Israel remains an essential component of the mystery. Through the centuries from Pentecost to parousia, the celebration of 'the mysteries' by the gathered Church in worship advances the kingdom and hastens the coming of the Lord. The depth of the mystery is further revealed in the calling of the Church to be the bride of the Lamb. Throughout this formation of the body of Christ, his own indwelling through his Spirit is decisive, as the Spirit prepares and purifies the bridal Church,

which already enjoys the 'hope of glory' (Col. 1:27).
Finally, the plan of God reaches its completion with
the sounding of the last trumpet, heralding the
coming of the Lord Jesus in glory and the
resurrection of the dead. Even reflection on the
'mystery of lawlessness' and the history of Babylon
heightens our awareness of the mystery of Christ,
that becomes the mystery of the bride and the
bridegroom, 'the holy city, new Jerusalem, coming
down out of heaven from God, prepared as a bride
adorned for her husband' (Rev. 21:2).

The Renewal of Catholic Life and Worship

To readers well acquainted with Catholic
terminology it will be evident that there are
similarities between the biblical use of the term
'mystery' and the common Catholic usage, but that
they are not identical. As mentioned in the
Introduction, mystery in the common Catholic
understanding refers to a truth or reality that is
inaccessible to human reason on its own and can
only be known by divine revelation.

Our reflection has shown how the biblical concept of
mystery expresses the purposefulness of God the

Creator. For Paul, mystery conveys an intense dynamism, the dynamism of the Holy Spirit, carrying the eternal project of God forward to its final accomplishment in Jesus Christ. Through the Christian centuries, as the Church settled down in the world, there was a loss of this eschatological dynamism. The 'blessed hope' of Christ's coming in glory became weakened, and for many - despite the profession of this hope in the Creeds of the Church - the Christian hope was effectively reduced to going to heaven when we die. As the hope for the kingdom weakened, the term 'mystery' came to be mostly restricted to supernatural truths that could only be known by divine revelation. By comparison with Paul's vision and language, this understanding is somewhat static.

The first major thrust to recover the biblical dynamism of the mystery came with the liturgical renewal of the twentieth century. From the beginnings of the modern liturgical movement in Belgium the focus was pastoral. The goal was to make the liturgy once again the living worship of the People of God. Liturgical scholarship was closely associated with the renewal of biblical studies, given the strong biblical character of liturgical language and symbolism. For this reason, the biblical apostolate was closely connected with the liturgical.[1]

As a result, the language of mystery was especially used in the context of the Church's liturgy, particularly with the phrase 'paschal mystery' referring to the Passover of the Lord in his death and resurrection. So, the *Catechism of the Catholic Church* at the beginning of its section on the liturgy and the sacraments states: 'He [Christ] accomplished this work [of redemption] principally by the Paschal mystery of his blessed Passion, Resurrection from the dead, and glorious Ascension, whereby "dying he destroyed our death, rising he restored our life". ... For this reason, the Church celebrates in the liturgy above all the Paschal mystery by which Christ accomplished the work of our salvation.'[2] This is in fact a return to the terminology regularly used by the Fathers of the Church.

The renewal of the liturgy goes hand in hand with the reappropriation of the 'blessed hope' of Christ's coming in glory. It is clearly expressed in most of the acclamations introduced after the consecration in the Mass.[3] In several striking paragraphs, the

Catechism of the Catholic Church speaks of the liturgy preparing for and even hastening the coming of the Lord. 'Since the apostolic age the liturgy has been drawn towards its goal by the Spirit's groaning in the Church: *Marana tha!*'[4] It is above all through the renewal of the liturgy that the Catholic Church is recovering the dynamism of mystery, that contains the fullness of the biblical hope.

The Ecumenical Challenge

As mentioned in the Introduction, there is a large segment of the Christian world that is uncomfortable with the term 'mystery' and rarely uses it. This is the world of the Evangelicals, which in this respect also includes the Pentecostals and independent charismatics. These are the Christians who particularly insist on everything being biblical; they are also the Christians who have paid most attention to the status of the Jewish people and the second coming of the Lord.

It will, I hope, be clear after the presentation of mystery in this book that a full reappropriation of the biblical perspective on mystery with its eschatological dynamism is essential for positive relationships between Catholics and Evangelicals, and indeed between liturgical and Free Church Christians. The Catholic rediscovery of the mystery in the New Testament sense can help to remove obstacles that prevent the Evangelicals from seeing the ways in which their lack of appreciation for mystery has weakened their own understanding of the Scriptures.

The charismatic movement has a valuable role to play in this coming together of Catholic and Evangelical. For its emphasis both on the Holy Spirit and on the Scriptures can render fuller justice to Paul's teaching on the 'unveiling' of the mystery through the Holy Spirit. The revitalization of liturgical worship through the charismatic impulse demonstrates how inherited liturgical forms and a genuine openness to the Holy Spirit are not mutually exclusive, but enrich each other.

Finally, the focus on mystery can provide a corrective for a major weakness in the charismatic movement. There is a tendency for those who have experienced the power and dynamism of the Holy Spirit to focus on short-term goals and to succumb to a hyper-intensive activism. The revelation of the mystery unveils the heart of the Father. The celebration of the mystery in the liturgy invites the Christian into the trinitarian communion of the Church. It makes possible a deeper contemplation of the mystery in the biblical sense, the full revelation of God in Jesus Christ. In this way, the Holy Spirit opens up the eternal perspectives of God, leading us into that combination of impatience and patience that characterizes the holy apostles and prophets of all generations. We are to have the impatience that burns with zeal for the Lord's purpose to be fulfilled ('how I am constrained until it is accomplished' Luke 12:50) and the patience that knows that everything including the timing is in the hands of the Father ('But of that day and hour no one knows, not even the angels of heaven, nor the Son, but the Father only' Matt. 24:36).

Jesus Christ came in the flesh. The glorified Jesus Christ now comes in the Spirit hidden under visible signs. Jesus Christ will come again visible in his glory. The mystery was manifested in Christ two thousand years ago. The mystery is always being revealed by the Spirit in the present of the Church. The mystery will be fulfilled: 'When Christ who is our life appears, then you also will appear with him in glory' (Col. 3:4).

NOTES

Chapter One

1. The coming of the Lord.
2. Para. 125.
3. One of the beatitudes had also spoken of the search for righteousness: "Blessed are those who hunger and thirst for righteousness, for they shall be satisfied." (Matt. 5:6).
4. See Amos 5:7; 6:12.
5. Other passages include: 'But the Lord of hosts is exalted in justice, and the Holy God shows himself holy in righteousness.' (Is. 5: 16). 'For as the earth brings forth its shoots, and as a garden causes what is sown in it to spring up, so the Lord God will cause righteousness and praise to spring forth before all the nations.' (Is. 61:11).
6. See also Ps. 53:2-3. These are among passages cited by Paul in Romans 3:10-18.

Chapter Two

1. *Evangelion* (Greek), *evangelium* (Latin), *évangile* (French).
2. See Acts 2:23-24; 3:13; 4:10; 5:30; 13:28-30.
3. See also Acts 13:30-39.
4. See Acts 13:26; Rom. 1:16; Eph. 1:13.

5. See also Phil. 2:14-16; 1 Thess. 5:23; Titus 2:11-13; James 5:8; 2 Peter 3:11-12; 1 John 2:28; Jude 24.

6. The Greek is *anomias*, the genitive of *anomia*, which is translated in the RSV as "lawlessness". The mystery of iniquity is treated in Chapter Thirteen at the end of this study.

7. See Chapter Ten for the revealing role of the Holy Spirit in the mystery of Christ.

Chapter Three

1. The Galilee appearance described in Matthew 28:16-20 may be an exception, as on this occasion it is said of the disciples that 'when they saw him they worshipped him' (v. 17).

2. See the section entitled 'First the Physical, Then the Spiritual' in Chapter Eight, and also Chapter Twelve on the resurrection of the body.

Chapter Four

1. See also Is. 49:22.

2. Among other passages that speak of the ingathering of God's scattered people are: Is. 27:12-13; 43:5-6; 60:4; Ez. 36:24; Ps. 147:2.

3. See Jer. 31:33-34; Ez. 11:19-20; 36:26-27.

4. See Ez. 38-39; Joel 3:1-3; Zech. 14: 2-3, 12.

5. See also Is. 56:6-7; 60:3; 62:2. This aspect is further developed in Chapter Seven.

6. 'The Beatitudes depict the countenance of Jesus Christ and portray his charity.' (CCC, para. 1717).

7. CCC, para. 1344.

8. 'I assign to you, as my Father assigned to me, a kingdom, that you may eat and drink at my table in my kingdom' (Luke 22:29-30). See also Chapter Eight.

9. Para. 780.

10. CCC. para. 674. The place of the Jews in the mystery of Christ is examined in Chapters Six and Seven.

11. The resurrection of the body is examined in Chapter Twelve.

Chapter Five

1. *The Glory of the Lord: Vol. VII: Theology: The New Covenant* (San Francisco: Ignatius Press, 1989), p. 205.
2. From the words of the Apostles' Creed.
3. See Chapter Ten.

Chapter Six

1. See Acts 9:15; 22:21; 26:17; Gal. 2:9.
2. Paul had already used the word 'stumble' to describe the Jewish rejection of Jesus: 'They have stumbled over the stumbling stone' (Rom. 10:32).
3. The Greek uses a different word *apobolē* in Rom. 11:15 from Rom. 11:1, which has *apōsato*. The French ecumenical translation TOB has *'mis à l'écart'* in verse 15, put aside.
4. This imagery is taken up again in Rev. 11:4.
5. Para. 674.
6. J. M. Lustiger *La Promesse,* p. 76 (author's translation).

Chapter Seven

1. E.g.: Is. 60:10-14; 61:5-6; 66:12, 20.
2. The 'we' and the 'our' in Isaiah 52:13 - 53:12 refer in context to the chosen people. 'But he was wounded for our transgressions, he was bruised for our iniquities; upon him the chastisement that made us whole, and with his stripes we are healed.' (53:5). This rather obvious fact is confirmed a few verses later: 'he was cut off out of the land of the living, stricken for the transgression of my people.' (53:8). See also Matt. 1:21: 'you shall call his name Jesus, for he will save his people from their sins.'
3. I say 'non-Jews' because there were 'proselytes', that is full Gentile converts to Judaism, present on the day of Pentecost (Acts 2:10) and one, Nicolaus of Antioch, among the seven 'deacons' in Acts 6:5.
4. See also Acts 11:15, 17.
5. The fact that the first disciples called Christians were Gentiles is

the biblical justification given by most Messianic Jews today for refusing the label 'Christian', which they say is only appropriate for Gentile believers.

6. In Greek, his name is *Jakobos*, so a more accurate English version would be Jacob.

7. The four requirements are: abstinence from animals sacrificed to idols, from blood, from what is strangled, and from *porneia* (generally translated as unchastity).

8. That is *sygklēronoma* (co-heirs), *syssōma* (joint body), *symmetocha* (co-sharers).

9. Another 'co' word, *sympolitai*.

10. See Chapter Ten on the role of the Holy Spirit in revealing the mystery.

Chapter Eight

1. Para. 1075.

2. 'the gospel concerning his Son, who was descended from David according to the flesh and designated Son of God in power according to the Spirit of holiness by his resurrection from the dead' (Rom. 1:3-4).

3. CCC, para. 610.

4. CCC, para. 1340.

5. CCC, para. 1076.

6. Decree on the Life of Priests, para. 4.

7. *Ecclesia de Eucharistia*, para. 18.

8. CCC, para. 1107.

Chapter Nine

1. See also Jer. 5:11.

2. See also Matt. 9:15; Luke 5:34-35.

3. Verses 25, 28, 29, 33.

4. 'as a plan for the fullness of time, to unite all things in him' (1:10) and 'he has put all things under his feet' (1:22).

5. 'until we all attain to the unity of the faith and of the knowledge of

the Son of God, to mature manhood, to the measure of the stature of the fullness of Christ' (4:13).

6. See Chapter Six.
7. See Chapter Seven.
8. John 2:4; 19:26.
9. See Chapter Thirteen.
10. Isaiah 65:17; 66:22; 2 Peter 3:13.

Chapter Ten

1. See Rom. 16:2, 15; 1 Cor. 16:15; 2 Cor. 1:1; Eph. 1:1; Phil. 1:1; Col. 1:2.
2. 'Faith is certain. It is more certain than all human knowledge because it is founded on the very word of God who cannot lie.' (CCC, para. 157).
3. Constitution on the Church, *Lumen Gentium,* para. 12.
4. Ibid., para. 12.

Chapter Eleven

1. See also Ps. 8.
2. See, for example: Is. 24:1-13; Jer. 3:2-4; 4:23-28; 12:4; Hosea 4:1-3.
3. See Chapter Twelve for more on the resurrection of the dead.

Chapter Twelve

1. Para. 998.
2. The phrase 'the day of the Lord' is used in 1 Thess. 5:2 and 2 Thess. 2:2 in the same sense as 'the day of [our Lord Jesus] Christ'.
3. See Luke 17:22, 25, 26. See also Matt. 24.
4. From prayer *Libera nos* that follows the Our Father in the Roman Liturgy.
5. The Catholic Catechism in its teaching on 'Marriage in God's Plan' has sections on 'Marriage in the order of creation', 'Marriage under the regime of sin', 'Marriage under the pedagogy of the Law', and 'Marriage in the Lord'. Para 1602-1617.

Chapter Thirteen

1. See 1 Thess. 2:18; 1 Tim. 4:1; Heb. 2:15; 1 Peter 5:8.
2. Para. 395.
3. Rev. 17:5; 18:2, 10, 21.
4. 'She who is at Babylon, who is likewise chosen, sends you greetings; and so does my son Mark.' (1 Peter 5: 13).
5. 'until the number of their fellow servants and their brethren should be complete, who were to be killed as they themselves had been.' (Rev. 6:11).
6. *Tertio Millennio Adveniente*, para. 37. See also John Paul II, *Veritatis Splendor,* paras. 90-94; *Ut Unum Sint,* paras. 83-84; *Incarnationis Mysterium,* para. 13; *Ecclesia in Europa,* para 13.
7. Para. 675.
8. Para. 677.

Epilogue

1. This was clear in the work of Fr Pius Parsch in Austria from the 1920s.
2. Para. 1067.
3. E.g. 'Christ has died, Christ is risen, Christ will come again.' 'Dying, you destroyed our death, rising you restored our life. Lord Jesus, come in glory.'
4. Para. 1130. See also paras. 1090, 1107, 1403, 2771, 2772.